REACHING MITHYMNA

By the Same Author

REACHING

MITHYMNA

Among the Volunteers

and Refugees on Lesvos

Steven Heighton

A John Metcalf Book

BIBLIOASIS
WINDSOR, ONTARIO

FIRST EDITION

Library and Archives Canada Cataloguing in Publication

Title: Reaching Mithymna : among the volunteers and refugees on Lesvos / Steven Heighton.
Names: Heighton, Steven, author.
Identifiers: Canadiana (print) 20200243241 | Canadiana (ebook) 2020024325X | ISBN 9781771963763 (softcover) | ISBN 9781771963770 (ebook)
Subjects: LCSH: Heighton, Steven, 1961– | LCSH: Refugee camps—Greece—Lesbos (Municipality) | LCSH: Refugees—Greece—Lesbos (Municipality) | LCSH: Syria—History—Civil War, 2011– —Refugees. | LCSH: Volunteer workers in social service—Greece—Lesbos (Municipality)
Classification: LCC HV640.4.G8 H44 2020 | DDC 362.87/83—DC23

Edited by John Metcalf
Copy-edited by John Sweet
Text and cover designed by Michel Vrana
Interior photographs copyright © Neal McQueen Photography

The poem "Christmas Work Detail, Samos," which appears on pp. 192–93, was first published in *The Moth* (Ireland), April 2019.

 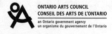

Published with the generous assistance of the Canada Council for the Arts, which last year invested $153 million to bring the arts to Canadians throughout the country, and the financial support of the Government of Canada. Biblioasis also acknowledges the support of the Ontario Arts Council (OAC), an agency of the Government of Ontario, which last year funded 1,709 individual artists and 1,078 organizations in 204 communities across Ontario, for a total of $52.1 million, and the contribution of the Government of Ontario through the Ontario Book Publishing Tax Credit and Ontario Creates.

PRINTED AND BOUND IN CANADA

Every heart, every heart
To love will come
But like a refugee.

—Leonard Cohen

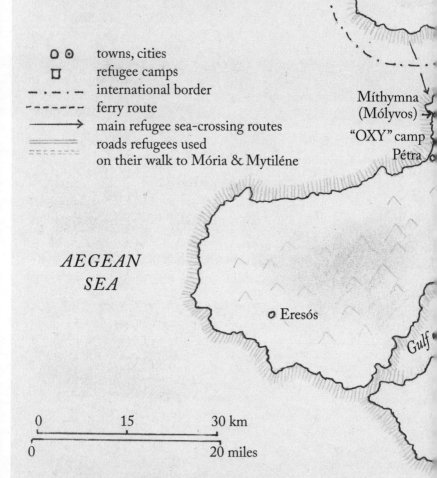

ISLAND OF
LESVOS / ΛΕΣΒΟΣ

○ ◉   towns, cities
⊓   refugee camps
— · — · —   international border
- - - - -   ferry route
———▶   main refugee sea-crossing routes
≡≡≡≡   roads refugees used
on their walk to Mória & Mytiléne

Míthymna
(Mólyvos)
"OXY" camp
Pétra

AEGEAN
SEA

○ Eresós

Gulf

0   15   30 km

0   20 miles

SH19

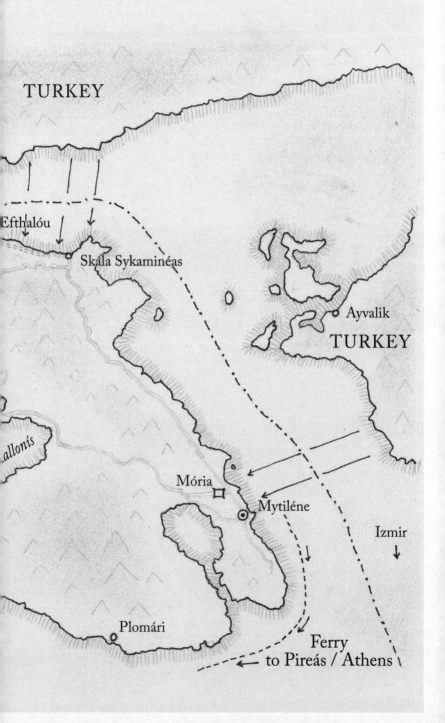

THE GREEK WORD FOR REFUGEES, *prosfyges*, BREAKS down etymologically into something like *toward-fleers*, or *those fleeing forward*—people not so much in flight from former homes as urgently seeking new ones. So the Greek noun erases the *prosfyges'* temporal and geographical past, as if to emphasize there is no returning, while at the same time it leaves the future indefinite, shoreless, an aspirational but as yet uncertain thing. To be a πρόσφυγας is to exist on an ever-vanishing cusp or border, the forward-moving edge of the raft-in-time.

This moment-by-moment limbo is everyone's dilemma (the past is dead, the future unborn, unguaranteed) but only the homeless fully inhabit it.

CONTENTS

A note on naming

THE NAMES OF THE VOLUNTEERS AND THE REFUGEES that readers will encounter in these pages have been changed to reflect the fact that each character is my approximation or re-creation of an actual person. Similarly, I refer to the town that has been the epicentre of the trans-Aegean refugee influx as Mithymna rather than Molyvos. (Mithymna, the town's ancient name, was revived in 1919 as its official modern name, but Molyvos—the Byzantine and Ottoman-era term—remains the one in general use.) Finally, I transliterate the name of the island on which the book is set as Lesvos, simply because modern Greek pronounces the letter beta (βήτα) as a *v*.

—S.H.

For Tracey, Omar, and Clara
who were there and still are

I. INITIATION

OCTOBER 30, 2015: *Authorities on the island of Lesvos, Greece, have announced that in the wake of Wednesday's sinking of a boat packed with over 300 migrants, the death toll has risen to 29. Many of the drowned were children and babies. The Hellenic Coast Guard reported that so far 274 people have been rescued from the sea off the island's northern coast. Local fishing boats participated in the rescue, ferrying survivors and the dying from a sinking boat to the harbour town of Molyvos (Mithymna), where paramedics and volunteers offered assistance and triaged ambulance transport. Many victims, suffering from shock or hypothermia, received first aid in a chapel on the pier.*

Lesvos continues to bear the brunt of the Syrian and Middle Eastern refugee influx. More than half a million people have reached the island so far in 2015, as many as 7,500 in a single day.

Border straits

THE ONLY OTHER PERSON ABOARD THE BUS, THE
driver, shakes me awake. I see myself in duplicate in his
aviator shades. "Mithymna?" I ask. He nods. His dangling
crucifix bears a crudely rendered Christ, the body skeletal,
the face large, plump and calmly self-satisfied.

Mumbling thanks, I pick up my bags and step down
onto the hot road. No traffic passing, not a living thing in
sight. Is it already the siesta hour? You'd never know this
part of the island was thronged with war refugees and that
hundreds, thousands more were arriving daily.

The bus stays put, idling, the driver slumped behind
the wheel as if already napping behind his sunglasses.
Nothing wants to be awake right now. I've barely slept
in fifty hours—an overnight flight, a second night on a

ferry—and as I close and rub my eyes, a montage of pre-sleep psychedelia starts looping.

Across the road, a town of whitewashed houses with terracotta roofs climbs the face of a high crag topped by a Crusader castle. On this side of the road, olive groves fall away downhill to a long rank of cypresses, the sea glistening beyond.

I turn onto a dirt lane and let the slope carry me down through the olive groves past a few shuttered houses, gaping work sheds, a weedy lot where the hulks of cars sit rotting. I pass between two cypresses and here is the seafront, a paved road running north-south along a narrow beach of white sand and pebbles. The shallows look tropically turquoise. Orange buoys bob offshore. The sea smells of kelp and something I can't place at first... associations of fear, distress... it's iodine, the intensely stinging stuff my mother painted onto cuts when I was small.

On the low seawall, beside a pack of Greek cigarettes and a half-empty water bottle, there's a coil of rope, some barbed steel hooks, and a cookie tin full of chicken feet the raw grey-pink of earthworms. Beyond them sits a white plastic pail. I look inside: a glutinous, translucent mass of octopods, motionless, though they give a faint impression of trembling.

No sign of the fisherman, who might be napping in some nearby shade.

I follow the paved road south along the beach. There are supposed to be hotels and rooms for rent down here. Off-season now they might be cheap, especially for someone who means to stay for a month. But the small places on either side of this T-junction are boarded up. The buildings to my left—two-storey hotels, cafés, clubs—are all shuttered. Would they normally be closed at this time of year or has the refugee influx damaged tourism even more than I've heard?

Something odd appears up ahead at the waterline. The sun in my eyes, I squint to focus. It looks like an immense sea animal, beached and decomposing, an elephant seal, a small whale.

I drop my bags and walk diagonally down the beach—a matter of a few steps—and continue along the water. As I approach the carcass I step over an orange life vest half-buried in wet sand and realize those buoys offshore must be life vests too. Of course. Now my eyes make sense of the wreckage ahead: a half-deflated dinghy, its black rubber snout aground on the beach, stern wallowing in the shallows.

I find the dinghy's aft section full of oily water. A red parka floats there, arms outstretched, amid empty water bottles, a plastic diaper and a few banknotes, maybe Syrian.

This vessel is no roomier than a large kiddie pool but will have ferried at least sixty people, reportedly the minimum the human smugglers will squeeze aboard.

I walk farther. Another dinghy is half-submerged some distance out and drifting shoreward. On the tideline and in the shallows, more life jackets, water bottles, disposable diapers, a saturated hoodie, an infant soother, cigarette butts.

Two sodden workboots, the laces loose and weed-twined.

A map turning to gruel in a plastic sandwich bag.

A green headscarf, the clasp pin still attached.

A tiny shoe with pink laces tied—surprisingly, since the sea is reputed to loosen and unknot everything, gradually undressing the drowned. Then again, any parent who has laced the shoes of a small child knows that you knot them with special care before embarking on a journey.

I plod back up to the road. The bus is gone. A sun-dried little man with a white-stubbled face sits on the bench there, leaning over his cane. I ask him where I can find a room. He turns his gaze up toward the castle, the almost parodically picturesque town. "You will climb the hill until you smell the hot bread," he says. "There you will find Elektra."

The white walls of these narrow cobblestone lanes and stairways redouble the light and the heat. My breath is ragged, sweat blurs my eyes. I stop to rest on a stone bench in the shade of a still-flowering trellis and consider the hand-lettered sign in a window across the lane: MUNICIPALITY CAFÉ OPEN. I'm parched and haven't had a solid meal in two days. I walk over and look in. As indicated by its unromantic name, the place is no tourist joint; a cluster of drably clad codgers hunches over some board game under a smog of pipe and cigarette fumes. The other wooden tables are free.

I sit a few steps from the men. Two are playing checkers while the rest hover close, watching from under hairy eyebrows, hailing certain moves with murmurs of approval, explosively protesting or debating others. They're drinking out of varied small glasses and smaller cups—ouzo or Greek coffee or wine. From the bar, a CD/cassette deck warbles out Greek songs. Above it, a quaintly executed mural shows a man dressed like the ones beside me—tattered blazer over wool sweater and dark fisherman's cap—seated beside a doctor in a lab coat. The doctor is administering a transfusion not from drip sacs of blood or saline but from a huge cask of ouzo. The caption, in stylized Cyrillic, is difficult to read, but it seems clear that the doctor is apologizing for any pain while the grinning fisherman replies that, on the contrary, he feels none.

A woman appears in an apron stained like a butcher's over a white blouse and jeans. She sets a double ouzo and a glass of water on my table and stalks off. Does she dispense a dose to every customer, or did she see me squinting at the mural and think that I, too, appeared to need something strong?

During the overnight flight I read that on Lesvos there is little or no viniculture—the island specializes in ouzo and olive oil. A splash of water and this ouzo clouds beautifully. It's good—subtler, less sweet than the liquid licorice you find outside Greece, which is just watered ethanol with flavouring. I shoot it back, unable to sip, not now.

She brings another and I thank her.

In any life, two impulses compete: the aspiration to be more awake—aware, intentional, passionate, engaged—and a longing for anaesthesis. The second drink's impact does seem intravenous, numbing me, scrambling my thoughts while also triggering flashes of surreal clarity. The island's silent interior seen from the bus window: millions of olive trees filling the valleys and cloaking the mountains, and one solitary wind-contorted tree high on a clifftop, like a claw. Then, by the shore, that jellied, clotted mass of octopods and the worm-pale chicken feet. Boots and shoes aground on the tideline like beach-toy boats.

The woman in her apron arrives with the English menu, its two pages dog-eared and blotchy with wine and oil. I knead my eyelids, waiting for her to leave and give me a minute. She stands tapping the toe of her sensible work shoe to a whirling instrumental.

In Greek I try ordering one of the dozen listed items (octopus, oddly, not among them).

"No, not have today," she says in English.

I try another.

"No, not today!"

I order a third item and she tilts her head back, blinks her eyes and clicks her tongue. "*Ohi, den to ehoume poté!*" *No, we never have that one!*

The men have gone silent and are watching openly. One of the players holds his checkers piece above the board. A bushy bandit's moustache conceals his mouth, but his eyes have a tickled glint. Maybe this routine is one that the men have heard often but still enjoy.

"How about the *kalamarakia*?" I ask.

"Only in the summer, of course!"

Is this the point where the few foreigners who stumble in here give up and walk down to the tourist strip? Still, our exchange is cheering me up. I set down the menu and say in Greek, "Well, what do you have?"

"This evening?" she asks.

"Naturally, yes!" I say, splaying my palms, trying to enter into the spirit of things. This effort pleases our audience, who nod and murmur as if to say, *Bravo, the foreigner now stands up for himself!*

"This evening," she says, "only the *barbounia*."

"*Barbounia*... that's mullet, right?"

"What else would it be?"

The men are delighted, chuckling gruffly.

"Is it local?" I ask, a feeble comeback and a foolish question, as she and I both realize at the same time. She doesn't bother to respond. The men look away, as if embarrassed for me. *He tried, the foreigner, but how much can you expect of them after all...?*

Then it hits me. Maybe she and the old men think I would prefer not to order the local fish. Online, before my all-but-overnight decision to come here, I read that the fishermen of Mithymna were struggling to sell their catch now that refugees were drowning in the border straits between Turkey and Lesvos. Local folks worried that the fish—octopods certainly included but, who knows, maybe also the mullet?—might be scavenging the flesh of the drowned.

The fishermen's losses struck me as a cruel irony, since many of them had been risking their lives sailing out into the fall gales whenever the overloaded rafts flooded or capsized. Their efforts had stirred in me feelings of a kind I've always viewed with distrust: ethnic identification and pride. In this case the sentiments seemed especially suspect, since my maternal grandparents had emigrated over a century before, and from a very different part of Greece—mountainous, landlocked—and I'd long since lost touch with any relatives there.

All the same, those feelings had helped decide me.

"I'll have the *barbounia*," I tell her and the men.

Minutes later she brings out a tumbler of cold red wine, half a loaf of warm bread in a basket, and a clay pitcher of olive oil. The oil is green and deliciously bitter. As I finish a third hunk of soaked bread, she brings out my meal, plunks it in front of me and says, curtly but not unkindly, "*Kali orexi.*" Bon appétit.

The three *barbounia* with their vitrified black eyes are coral pink. With my knife tip I pry open the largest one's mouth: the toothless upper jaw of a vegetarian. Beside it, a steaming heap of *horta*—parboiled winter greens in oil, lemon juice, sea salt—and rosemary potatoes roasted with garlic and lemon. A simple dinner, in fact like childhood meals from the years before my late mother retired her recipes and assimilated to North American suburbia, Etobicoke.

The young wine is fresh and tart, the potatoes browned on the outside and creamy within. Between mouthfuls I hear myself sigh. To be overtaken by gratitude in this rare way is almost painful. It is painful, and the shock of sleepless arrival in a real place is only part of the cause; Lesvos is also a crisis zone, a crime scene, and the one length of shoreline I've walked is a cenotaph.

Still, I'm slower to cut into the walleyed fish, warily filleting as if I'll discover something other than bones.

I look up. Did the men hear me sigh, notice me staring at my plate? Their faces are averted, hat brims lowered toward the game board. To them, I might be another Greek of the diaspora, back in the mother country, emotional over his first meal. Finding that perfectly natural, they've chosen to grant me a respectful privacy.

I climb on up the slope, the sun lower and shaded by the leafy trellises sheltering the lane. At last a fragrance of fresh bread hurries me on and I stoop through a low doorway into a neolithic-looking stone hive. Winded, I nod to the yawning teenager behind the counter.

"You are just in time," she says in English. "We are closing. You are a volunteer?"

"I'd like to be. I hear you need some."

"We need many."

I drop the bags and point to the last loaf on the shelf behind her. "And do you know where I can find Elektra?"

"Of course. You are very close." She leads me outside and points up the street at a shingle above a door: ELEKTRA GASTHAUS.

The owner is a burly woman with henna-dyed hair, operatic eyeliner and a shrewdly appraising gaze. As I stand in her doorway she pumps my hand like a football coach, then half turns and presents her husband, Alexis, a red-faced man in a watch cap sitting behind her in the shadows at a hulking old desktop computer.

I'm surprised to meet a husband, since Elektra's house-dress, scarf, and slippers are widow-black.

She leads me up an outside stairway onto a concrete veranda and into a dim, drafty hallway. "The first three rooms are taken by other volunteers," she says in Greek, "but the back one is unoccupied." Unlocking the door she adds, "I can speak some German, but poorly."

"I'm sure mine is worse."

"You aren't German? Most of the volunteers…"

"Actually I'm half-Greek, on my mother's side."

She eyes me, as if weighing whether or not to make some remark, probably about my Greek. I drop my luggage and enter the room: a double bed, sink, small fridge and stove with gas burners, a tiny bathroom and, through the sliding door, another, private veranda with a sunlit table and chair. Above the table, pomegranates droop among waxy leaves. She names a price and eyes me sidelong, her pencilled eyebrows raised; she expects me to quibble. But it's cheap, cheaper than I'd hoped for, and I'm too tired to bargain. I tell her I'll take it for a month.

Fifteen minutes later, a sharp rapping on the door, which swings open. Stripped to shorts and an undershirt, chewing a piece of bread, I'm hanging shirts in the wardrobe. Elektra sweeps in, cradling a stuffed paper bag. "Here are things to eat," she says in German. And then, in Greek, "The volunteer men never feed themselves properly." On the Formica table beside my half-eaten loaf she sets out a packet of Greek coffee, clear bags of pistachios and almonds, a slab of cheese in wax paper, tins of sardines, ripe tomatoes and apricots, a pocket bottle of ouzo and three packs of Marlboros. There's also a plastic water bottle filled with a viscous liquid resembling motor oil. She flourishes the bottle and blurts something. I spread my hands, grinning stupidly, and she re-explains as rapidly as before but with extra words and exaggerated gestures: it's fresh olive oil, the very best virgin oil, pressed this very morning down at the farmers' collective. "You must never again eat your bread dry," she rebukes me, "as if this is a time of poverty or war."

The Captain's Kitchen

FROM WHERE I'M LYING, THE ONE VISIBLE PATCH OF sky, through the branches of the pomegranate tree, seems a darkening panel of violet glass. I must have slept several hours. Jet lag presses me down into the mattress as if the force of gravity has tripled, and there's the hollow, hungover feeling of waking not as the sun returns but after it has set.

Predictably it begins, a murmur I've spent years suppressing, ignoring, medicating with exercise and less wholesome drugs, distracting with plans, achievements, minor changes and other useful turmoils. A verdict lodged under the floorboards of dailiness, lying in wait for illness, doubt, shame, insomnia or simply times when the ego, in its armour of agendas, lets down its guard. Then the voice whispers its bitter nothings, revising *onward* to *noward, noneward, unward.*

I'm still not sure why I'm here, beyond a wish to do something useful, involving flesh and blood people instead of invented characters and words on a screen. Three nights ago on the phone with my daughter—nineteen and now living away from home—I'd mentioned my impulse and then thought: Let's see you act for a change, not just pipe-dream and make principled noises; not just *write* about Mediterranean refugees in a novel, as I was then doing.

Still, I doubted I would go. I would convince myself it was too expensive (it wasn't, off-season and owing to how the crisis had gutted tourism); I would balk at cancelling several paid commitments; I would tell myself the next draft of my overdue novel couldn't wait a month; I would feel guilty leaving my wife solely in charge of our old, in fact dying, dog, whose care had been mainly my job.

I will myself up and take a cool shower. Cool or cold seem to be the only choices. I brew a Greek coffee, extra strong, following the instructions on the packet. I mean to walk down to the harbour and find a place called the Captain's Kitchen. Hours before leaving for Greece I'd received an email reply from an old friend with Lesvos connections, who'd told me the restaurant was now also the headquarters of a refugee aid foundation that needed volunteers.

I pick my way through meandering dark alleys until I hit a wider, lamplit lane running straight downhill to the lower town. There are lighted windows here and there, a few people in cafés or corner stores, but mostly the town is quiet.

In the harbour a north wind is sweeping over the break-water and along the pier. The fishing boats moored there wobble, groan and creak. The restaurants are shuttered and dark except for the one whose sign says *Captain's Kitchen*. Its roofed front porch—winterproofed with roll-down panels of clear plastic—glows invitingly. The only life out here is a handful of cats sitting along the pier's edge, on piles of netting and coiled hawsers, as if waiting for a boat to come in with fish. But surely no fishing boats—or rubber dinghies—are out there in the dark, in this wind?

I approach the covered porch. In its warmly lit bubble a half-dozen young people in bright-coloured multi-wrap scarves sit together, faces separately aglow in the screen light of laptop computers or cellphones. At a corner table, a slightly older woman studies her laptop. It's like I'm peering through the window of a university library on a winter's night, my collar raised against the wind. A small figure appears beside me: a woman bent under a stuffed-to-bursting mountaineer's backpack larger than she is. Her high-cheekboned face and her shoulders are dwarfed by a mass of frizzy curls. She's a Merchant Ivory heroine but in high-top sneakers and shapeless parka and with a cigarette drooping from her lips.

"You going to volunteer with them?" she asks in a cracked, husky voice, her accent unplaceable.

"I guess so. You?" I nod at her backpack. "You just arrived?"

Wind sweeps away the smoke she puffs out. "Oh, man, none of this is mine. If I'm coming from Oslo, I might as well bring them warm things, eh? They"—she nods toward the restaurant—"they do a good job of sharing it out. They're a new outfit, but they're OK."

"So you volunteer with them? You're Norwegian?"

"No, man, Syrian. I live in Oslo now. I'm a translator. I work with a lot of groups. It's Fara."

I follow her up the steps into the covered porch, where a couple of the scarved volunteers leap up, greet her in German-accented English and help her get the backpack off. A space heater whirrs over the skirling of Greek pop. Through the restaurant doorway, behind a steam table, an aproned man in a hairnet works. I smell fish grilling and eggplant frying. Fara booms, "Hey, Lindsay, I think Steve here wants to join you."

The woman at the corner table looks up from her screen. Her wide-set eyes are red and unfocused. She's holding a cellphone. Short fair hair streaked mauve. Beside the laptop, a pouch of tobacco, papers, and a saucer full of crumpled butts. She beckons me over. In a barely audible voice she asks questions, then listens to my answers with an air of patient, intelligent sadness, her head slightly bowed. She holds the phone away from her but still poised.

"Sorry for the mobile," she says, and I think I get her accent—Yorkshire. "We're waiting for word from the coast guard. Are you available immediately, Steve?"

"I guess I am, sure."

She starts rolling a cigarette with one hand, fingers quick, nimble, the rest of her unmoving. A metallic voice chirps out of the phone and she claps it back to her head, gives me a slight nod and half turns away. "Yes, still here. Sorry...? All right. Half an hour...? I think so. And we've a new volunteer with us. Thanks." She sets down the phone, lights up and inhales. "We were told to expect a quiet night, with this weather. But a hundred Syrians just tried to get across. Coast guard and a fishing boat have gone out to bring them in. Fara, can you stay and help Asim with the passports?"

"No, man, I got to go out to Skala. They need a translator, some medical thing."

Lindsay shakes her head. "And I sent a few people home early—they were all night at OXY." She looks up at me. I hear the volunteers behind me pushing back chairs, snapping laptops closed, zipping daypacks. "Do you mind, Steve? Doing the passports? Some of the refugees get nervous when the passport person is too young. Asim will show you how—I'm calling him down from OXY— OXY's our camp." She picks up her cellphone.

"Of course," I say.

I have no idea what I've just agreed to.

Outside, I help Lindsay, along with the scarved young Germans and a Catalonian woman, Pilar, to move supplies to the head of the pier: crates of bottled water, packaged thermal sheets, sweaters and hats from a storage-bin depot behind the restaurant. We also bring up two of the heavy outdoor tables and two chairs, and, Lindsay indicating the spot, place them under one of the high dock-lamps. "You'll be sitting here, Steve." I can barely hear her; the winds are increasing, waves booming on the outer wall of the breakwater that hides the sea from view. Lamplit spray explodes above it.

She hurries back toward the restaurant, talking into her phone.

A droning rumble emerges over the roar of the waves and now an aura glows above the breakwater, as if the moon is about to rise. The coast guard ship, I assume. I have no idea what to do and there is no one here to ask. The others are scrambling around the pier like novices, which maybe they are. Back beyond the restaurant, car headlights descend the road from town, presumably reinforcements.

If this moment seemed fully real, I might be panicking.

The spotlit upper deck of a coast guard cutter slides along the pier's outer arm and then, rounding the green beacon, enters the harbour. Briefly it slices straight toward us, engines howling as if at ramming speed; back in front of the restaurant the cats are scattering. But now the ship slows down, veering and pulling in along the inside of the outer arm, across the harbour.

Lindsay returns with a slender, pale man, maybe twenty-five, close-cropped Caesar haircut and shy, almost self-erasing manner. The cotton bib over his parka reads TRANSLATORS WITHOUT BORDERS. She makes introductions—Asim, Steve—and she's gone. Asim offers me a few printed sheets and a ballpoint pen. In an East London accent with a slight stammer, he explains that he'll be receiving the people without passports or with Arabic documents; I'll be receiving the rest. Having been rescued by the coast guard after entering Greek waters, the refugees are deemed to be under arrest until officially registered.

Incredibly, official registration is going to involve a jet-lagged rookie sitting at a café table under a flickering lamp with a chewed pen and a form that seems to have been composed on a typewriter and copied on a machine short of ink. Down the left margin run numbers, 1 to 40. Across the top: NAME, FATHERNAME, BIRTHDAY, NATIONALTY, PASSPORT #.

I call to Asim, who's sitting at his own table: "Is there some kind of, uh, official vest I can put on over this?" Besides my motorcycle jacket I'm wearing a black toque, blue jeans and drill boots, like the informal border guard of some post-apocalyptic pseudo-state. "I don't want to alarm them—I mean, asking for their passports."

"Alarm them?"

"She said they get uncomfortable with some volunteers—I guess if they seem unofficial."

"They won't be alarmed, mate," he says gently. "Not after what they've seen."

Two volunteers are sorting sweaters into piles by size, others tearing open packets to remove silver thermal wraps. Now a voice calls, "They are here!"

Led by what must be a coast guard official, the refugees are filing toward us along the breakwater through overlapping cones of lamplight. Fiction or film would depict shambling survivors, waiflike children, gimping elders falling behind. Nobody is falling behind. Whether afraid of lagging or simply attempting to stay warm, the whole group advances briskly.

Asim stands up, raises one hand and hollers some phrase in Arabic, this effort deforming his mild voice into a curt stranger's. Without a word the column splits obligingly, almost eagerly, into two single-file queues. Asim questions the first man in his group—gaunt, unshaven—while a line of shivering people bears down on my table.

First comes a man with white-whiskered nostrils and inflamed eyes. He frowns down at me. I try to take the passport he holds. He grips harder. Hoping to allay his fears—assuming his grip is not a hypothermic spasm—I smile and say, "*Marhabaan*." Welcome.

He lets go. I take and open the soggy booklet and transfer details onto the form. I return it to him with a "*Shukhran, salam!*"—thank you, peace be with you—thus exhausting the Arabic vocabulary I memorized on the ferry last night. He nods, still looking dubious, and moves on.

A family surges up as if pulled forward into a vacuum. The smallest child, a girl, is first to the table. Her rosebud nose bubbles and her teeth rattle. On either side of the line, volunteers are wrapping people in crinkling sheets that resemble tinfoil, offering hats, mittens, bottled water. Asim's voice murmurs questions steadily. He is standing with his clipboard, jotting details. Both lines are orderly and uncannily silent, but the refugees' taut, forward-tilting postures suggest a spring-loaded impulse to *move*, and in just one direction—onward, past this seat-of-the-pants customs post and into shelter.

I register the family quickly. The girl with the bubbling nose and cavernous black eyes edges past me, gaping as if I'm a phantom in a fever. She is pinching her thermal wrap closed at the throat with grubby fingers.

An old man with a priestly beard, in a Peruvian toque that a volunteer must have given him, tenders a passport he has protected against the sea with plastic wrap. I hold it to my eyes in the lamplight, then scratch at the tight layers—as if it has been commercially shrink-wrapped several times over. I try gouging with my thumbnail but can get no purchase. The queue splays wider as people push forward behind the old man, watching me. They start talking over each other, maybe offering me advice, maybe scolding the man for overprotecting the thing. I try using the sleeve-clip of the pen's cap to saw into the wrapping. No good.

The frustration in the queue is mounting. "Asim, do you have a pocket knife? Does anyone have a knife?" A young volunteer runs to get one from the Captain's Kitchen. Asim calls something in Arabic and a teenager emerges from behind the red-faced man and hands me a damp pen-knife. The man—in that infantilizing toque with its toggles and pompom—says nothing, but the others are jabbering instructions, encouragement. Their eyes gleam with impatience, though in other circumstances they might be amused. My own face must be red too, my nape and ears blazing. Even with the blade—and not a dull one—it's a struggle, but finally I carve through what must be a dozen layers of wrapping, then stab and hack free the passport while people in the line let out a relieved, tired cheer.

Forty minutes later, the coast guard cutter and two fishing boats arrive with a second, larger group of Syrians. Lindsay takes over at the passport table; Pilar and I are detailed to lead sixty of the first group up from the pier and through Mithymna to a rendezvous with a bus waiting on the far side of town. Buses can't squeeze through the town's narrow streets to the harbour, so the refugees have to walk to the vehicle that tonight will take them, I'm told, past the already-full OXY camp and on to a much larger camp called Moria.

Darren, a fit little Welshman vibrating with vexation, informs me that the walk to the bus is about two and a half kilometres, maybe half an hour. He was off-duty tonight but rushed down, he said, when he heard what was happening. "No fucking leisure in this holiday paradise, boyo. But you should have seen October. The fucking Greeks here are broke as tinkers. It was skeleton crews the whole way." His ruddy face gleams with sweat despite the cold winds. "The volunteerlings are going back to their schoolbooks now, good riddance. Nice to see another big-pants man turn up. Right, listen." He tosses off directions to the bus pickup. When I say the walk sounds long for people who have just been rescued from a sinking dinghy, he replies, "This is nothing, boyo. Till October they had to walk all the way to fucking Moria. Thirty miles right across the island."

My look of surprise brings a gratified gleam to his eye—the veteran inducting the rookie into the realities of the front lines. "Still," I say, "some of the children and old folks…"

"You expected, what, a mini tour-train? A funicular? Chauffeured limos? In October, we hadn't a fucking thing here. And these bastards are *tough*."

The directions sound, as directions always do, straightforward. The bus will be waiting in a parking lot beside the playing fields south of the town. *You can't fucking miss it, boyo.* Pilar, unlike me, has a cellphone, so in theory we could GPS our way there, but apparently Google Maps has been directing other parties to the wrong parking lot. So, spoken directions. I've received them, so I will lead and Pilar will bring up the rear, in case people fall behind.

Like Lindsay, she chain-smokes cigarettes she hand-rolls. Halting English, heavy accent. She tells me she became a volunteer only three days ago. Smiling on one side of her mouth, puffing smoke, she croaks, "OK, we are ready!"

"This way," I call out, waving my hand. As if I pass for a trained guide—a legitimate authority who knows the town and our destination beyond it—the densely packed group follows without hesitation. They walk resolutely, almost marching, as they did after disembarking from the rescue ship. Their various clothes—long tunics, scarves, jeans or slacks, ragged blazers, hoodies, parkas—are mostly dark. A few of them sport thermal blankets like shiny superhero capes. Anyone not in a hijab has some kind of winter hat now. Their belongings they lug over the shoulder in black garbage bags, and each family has at least one, while the single men carry either a daypack or nothing at all.

I head uphill away from the harbour along the pave-stoned main road. To our left: the steeply rising tiers of the town and, high above it, the heroically footlit castle. To our right: a chest-high stone wall above a rock face plunging to the sea. The road climbs steeply and I feel it in my thighs and worry again about the children and the older, or sicker, or wearier adults, but every time I look back, they're all moving well. The encouragements I instinctively call—*this way... almost to the top!*—are, to them, both incomprehensible and unnecessary.

I offer to take a stuffed garbage bag from a hunched woman who looks too small and tired to carry it (her hus-band cradles a dozing toddler, maybe a grandchild, swaddled in a man's jacket). Will she trust me? She hands it over instantly. I prop the bag on my right shoulder and brace it with my hand, feeling dampness through the plastic.

Every minute or so I pivot and walk backward a few steps, facing the group. When I catch a glimpse of Pilar, I wave and she waves back, cigarette between her fingers, the burner a tiny beacon. *All well!* Darren advised me not to let the group bunch up and clog this narrow main street, so now I'm signalling and calling, "Move over, please, *shukhran!*" Cars and scooters squeeze by at an unhellenically tolerant pace. Peaceably enough, old men with worry beads look on from streetside coffee houses and teenagers watch from the tables of fast-food joints. But then a driver accelerates furiously past us, his face gargoyled with rage.

After twenty minutes or so we reach the edge of town: the final café, the last few street lights, the bus stop where, impossibly, I stepped down barely seven hours ago. Our route has been simple thus far, straight south along the main street. Now we need to make a left turn. I assume this fork must be the place—a road angling off to the southeast and climbing into darkness. I pivot and announce our turn with what I hope will sound like veteran nonchalance. "This way—yes—please be careful—stay to the side!"

When you're trying to follow rough directions, the anxiety that you might have missed a turn or overshot your goal slows time to a quantum crawl. A ten-minute walk, especially in the dark, can seem like an hour as you scan both sides of the road with fading confidence. Every minute might be taking you farther in the wrong direction. You glance again at the instructions, if they're written down, or you try to recall them word for word. You can't. Idiot, why didn't you just listen *carefully* for once in your life? Maybe you fume about whoever gave you the directions, his casual vagueness, her lazy impatience in describing a route she herself could sleepwalk.

This anxiety feels a lot like full panic when you're trying to guide sixty chilled, hungry people who have already had to be rescued once tonight.

As the road ahead disappears into darkness, a puzzled murmuring starts up behind me. I notice I've slowed down. I shift the garbage bag to my other shoulder, feeling the clammy chill through my jacket and sweater. I turn and walk backward. Behind the steadily advancing refugees, the lights of Mithymna, crowned by its castle, are receding. Two men call out in worried, questioning voices and I call back, "Soon, soon—almost there!", which might or might not be a lie and anyway will mean nothing to them. I check my glowing watch. Thirty minutes' walk, Darren told me. Somehow we're only at twenty-five. *Thanks a fuck of a lot for the directions, man. You couldn't have come along, my first time?* The road is turning, descending, the lights of the town setting behind the hill. Pilar must be back there somewhere. Does she too assume I know where we're going?

I keep looking to the right; according to my marching orders an expanse of playing fields and basketball courts should be opening there, and across those fields a bus should be waiting. Instead I see—sense as much as see—a slope of olive trees falling away from the roadside. We've picked up speed, walking downhill, which should be encouraging—we're making progress! we'll be there soon!—but this momentum merely adds to my panic that I'm leading them ever farther from safety. The muttering behind me increases. I decide to say nothing, simply lead them faster—maybe doubling down on my mistake? Sweat prickles into my armpits. There's an open area of some kind to our right now (the fields?), but I can't be certain and there's no sign of a bus.

I plod on, barely able to see my feet, not to mention the road. A minor eternity of minutes. Finally—just as I start talking to myself, "Right, of course, you would screw up already, you *would* lead sixty freezing survivors into the middle of nowhere"—in the darkness ahead a large object erupts into life with a terrifying roar. The bus's windows and acetylene-white, red and yellow headlights, sidelights, rooflights all ignite like a festooned Christmas pavilion, or the mother ship ready to lift off. Cries of relief and joy surge up behind me and I exhale, "Thank God."

Accidental paramedic

THE VOLUNTEERS OF THE CAPTAIN'S KITCHEN ARE
responsible for two other zones besides Mithymna harbour:
a refugee landing and staging area at Efthalou Beach, just
east of the town, and a transit camp known by the name of
the nightclub in whose parking lot it sprawls: OXY. This
club is built into the face of a crag beside the highway a
few kilometres south of town. A high balcony—for sunset-
viewing, drinking and dancing—juts out of the crag like the
prow of a party boat. It looks down across the highway and
the guardrailed cliff, a thousand-foot drop to the Aegean.
Across the Bay of Petra, Lesvos recedes westward cape by
cape, while to the north the Turkish coast is a beautifully
bleak sierra of dust-coloured peaks.

No refugee camp in the world could enjoy finer views
or more ravishing sunsets.

The nightclub is closed for renovations, but no signs of work are apparent. Is the reno exclusively internal or is it another victim of the ongoing Greek economic debacle, which the refugee influx is now compounding? For the time being, the club's owners have agreed to let volunteers convert its unpaved, sloping parking lot into the OXY Transit Camp. Several NGOs have contributed supplies; the acronym of the United Nations Human Crisis Relief group is blazoned as patently as a corporate logo across the white plastic walls of the two huge, square tent shelters centring the camp. Smaller tents—some branded Red Cross or MSF, and others, in pine green or camouflage, furnished by the Greek army—surround the main shelters. There's also a white-painted plywood lavatory shed with stalls, urinals, sinks and an outside washing station for dishes and clothing.

The camp began as a simple rest stop where refugees, having just crossed the straits from Turkey, could lie down and sleep before the next stage of their journey, southward down the highway to the main camp at Moria. There they would be formally registered by the Greek authorities before going on to the island's capital, Mytilene, to board a ferry for the mainland. Their eventual goal was northern Europe, especially Germany.

By the time of my first shifts at OXY, many systems—relatively new but, to novice eyes, seeming solidly established—were in operation. For one, scores of repurposed tour buses came and went each day, shuttling newly arrived refugees to OXY from Efthalou Beach, or else picking them up at OXY to transfer them to Moria. But—as the excited Darren insisted on the pier—it hadn't been this way for long. Money to commandeer buses had only recently become available and the Greek military had never had enough trucks, or for that matter fuel, to transport hundreds or thousands of people a day.

Six thousand was the number on the heaviest day of the crisis, in late July—so I learned during my first OXY shift. I heard that after one of those lyric Aegean sunsets, the passengers of over a hundred inflatable dinghies lay down to rest on the gravel under the parking lot lights, while twenty volunteers tried and failed to provide each person with a processed cheese sandwich and a bottle of water. The toilet shed had not yet been built. Those in need had to scramble up the crag behind the shuttered nightclub or, after climbing the highway guardrail, hunker among the rocks and gorse along the clifftop.

Next morning they set out on foot. The Mediterranean sun would have launched its daily offensive by 5:30 a.m. and by noon the heat on the asphalt road would have been scorching. On that day—as on many others—the line of march would have straggled for hours along the highway, narrowing it to one lane. Some wore flip-flops and some walked barefoot, having to carry the shoes that had blistered and bloodied their feet. Some had no shoes to carry. Some hefted garbage bags of clothing, some shouldered children, some bore only the clothes on their backs.

Volunteers helped as best they could, setting up water stops along the route like road-race marshals. Still, by sunset many walkers, dehydrated and also famished, were weaving like drunks and there were near misses and a few collisions with local traffic that had luckily, like most of the cars in Mithymna, slowed down. Somehow no one was killed, not on that day or any other. And though most of the summer's

300,000 walkers, many of them children and old folks, accomplished the marathon in a day, no one died of the heat or a heart attack.

As for those who couldn't reach Moria by dark, they lay down for the night along the side of the road.

The camp is all but empty this evening—my third shift as a volunteer and second here at OXY. For hours the volunteers have been gathering refugees into groups of sixty, issuing tickets, managing lines, filling seats, and waving as the buses rumble out of the parking lot onto the highway. Just one extended family will overnight here, in a shelter where last night hundreds of people slept. (On the day's final bus there were a few empty seats, but the rule is never to split up families to fill a bus.)

Besides the ten Syrians now sitting on straw mats and eating a meal prepared in the mobile kitchen by cooks I haven't yet seen, only a handful of volunteers are present. The camp would be silent if not for the chugging generator and the soundtrack being piped through a small but Napoleonically assertive Fender amp. Tonight the playlist is a medley of crooner tunes, "New York, New York," "Fly Me to the Moon," and now "Mack the Knife." Since the last bus's departure, the volume has been dialed lower. When the family bed down in their circus-sized tent, it will be turned off.

The sound of a large vehicle gear-grinding into the parking lot drowns out "Mack the Knife." The bus is arriving from the north, Mithymna, the beaches. A second bus shudders in behind it and for some reason its headlamps—high beams?—are much brighter, as shocking and invasive as helicopter searchlights. The bus doors huff open and refugees emerge and stream downhill into the camp. Volunteers scramble to their stations: the men's and women's clothing tents and footwear tents, the canteen, the sleeping shelters. The camp is understaffed because—as on my first night—the word from certain "contacts" on the Turkish side was to expect no more arrivals until morning. So a number of volunteers have driven south to Moria to help out there overnight, while others have gone back into town for supper.

The remaining crew is instantly overwhelmed.

One of the rafts that just landed was repeatedly swamped and barely made it ashore, so its passengers are drenched to the skin. In front of the men's dry-clothing tent, under a string of light bulbs, men and boys are milling, some so cold they move with a spastic jerkiness, their teeth audibly chattering. No trace of the patient queues I've been seeing until now. Many of these people can't and won't wait. Behind fold-out tables at the front of the army tent, two volunteers—Klaus, a Buddhist in drawstring yoga pants and Biblical sandals, and I, on clothing detail for the first time—have braced for impact. There is no impact. Men simply flow past on either side of us. They're careful not to brush against us, meet our eyes, notice our raised palms, hear our pleas. Nothing aggressive in this incursion, their body language signals; nothing personal.

"Please, one at a time," Klaus keeps repeating in a sort of resigned sigh. I glance over my shoulder, thinking maybe a dozen refugees are behind us. The dim light bulbs dangling in the tent now show at least twice that number, rifling through the cardboard boxes and plastic bins, writh-ing out of their sodden things and hastily re-dressing. A teenager—balanced on one shivering leg—topples as he tries to wriggle into a pair of too-tight jeans. A skinny older man is pulling a second wool sweater down over a first. I walk toward him, saying, "Please, no, just one sweater!" Feeling invisible and inaudible, I'm surprised when he seems to understand me, removing the surplus sweater without protest.

From the women's clothing tent I hear Pilar in her heavy accent calling for the translator, Asim. Somebody yells back that he left an hour ago. Now Dieter and Oskar—the brusque, fussy German couple who usually supervise the men's tent—appear, towering above the crowd as they push toward us. They've returned from a restaurant in town to help. Dieter takes in the chaotic scene behind us. His Adam's apple bobs as if he has swallowed a golf ball. "You have not understood my instruction?" Spiked platinum hair, a rainbow patch on his coat shoulder. He directs a curt German phrase at the unprovocable Klaus—who nods mutely as if accepting a temple master's edict—while Oskar tells me coldly, "I think Omiros will be needing you at the canteen now. We take over here."

Kanella, a stray dog who has made a home in the camp, yammers and growls from the door of the canteen hut. She is slender, skittish; floppy ears, cinnamon fur, white socks. "It's all good, girl," I call as I approach, though from a canine viewpoint there can be little good in crowds of strangers encroaching on your territory day after day. The canteen may be the first secure food source and warm shelter she has known. Yesterday I saw her pacing the camp perimeter, mining it with drops of urine, a hormonal frontier invisible to us but real enough to any dog—and in fact chemically detectable. Which in a way makes it realler than any number of unmarked human borders, those figments that we kill for or risk our lives to cross.

"We will put her inside," Omiros calls to me as the two of us converge on the canteen. "The refugees, I think they fear dogs." His open leather trenchcoat flares behind him as he stalks along. His black boots crunch in the gravel. No one is sure of his real name, but the Greeks call him 'Omiros—Homer. He's six-three and brawny, but—unlike Anglo-American alpha males, who hulk and lumber as if chronically stiff from the weight room—his movements are light, fluent as a soccer star's or salsa dancer's. Nor does he squint or harden his soft brown eyes when addressing you. Yet his sympathetic gaze is offset by more conventional male markers: a balding head shaved bare, a black goatee nattily groomed. Syrian on his father's side, Spanish on his mother's, he has the tragically dashing looks of an Othello, or—in that oxblood trenchcoat like a villain's cape—the scene-seizing baddie in a film thriller. He would be the enemy with an anima and a backstory of deprivation: some galvanizing early grief. His order-restoring fall and death we would mourn more than we realize—though the film's backers would realize it and commission his resurrection in a sequel.

"Steve," he calls, "Stavro, come help me now!" Volunteers run past us, some toward the mobile kitchen, some returning from the supply room with thermal and wool blankets. Long shadows cast by the floodlights above the bus-loading lanes streak across the compound. The wind has risen and the high walls of the UNHCR tents ripple and snap. A sense of terrific animation fills the scene.

I follow Omiros behind the clothing tents, where another bus has just arrived, and we intercept a party descending toward us—Asim; a squat, bearded bus driver; and a heavy woman sprawled back in a wheelchair, her scarved head lolling. Asim and the driver are struggling to restrain the wheelchair on this grade. As we meet them, I realize the woman is unconscious.

"What is wrong with her?" Omiros asks, raising his voice over the wind.

"We don't know," Asim says. "She disembarked from the raft, but then on the bus..."

"What is 'disembark'?" Omiros asks.

"I must return," the driver says in Greek. "Others are waiting."

"I'll go back, help Lindsay," Asim mumbles. "I'll stay here once we bring up the rest. Iraqis." His lips barely move, like a ventriloquist's. They say he has hardly slept in weeks.

Omiros and I take the wheelchair, one handle each. We too struggle to restrain it and then—the slope levelling out—to push and steer it over the gravel. Finally we shove in through the door flaps of the military field tent that serves as medical clinic. A single light bulb dangling by a cord sways over a table. A few unoccupied cots. A portable radiator, searing to the touch. The Médecins Sans Frontières nurse must be off helping somebody who has collapsed or grown hypothermic.

Omiros and I consider trying to lift the bulky woman off the wheelchair onto a cot but decide it would be too difficult and risky. We leave her slumped in the chair, which we park and brake beside the radiator, in the corner farthest from the door flaps. "Wait with her," he says. "Check her signals."

"Her vital signs?"

"Her heart, her thermature."

"I'm no paramedic," I say.

"I will find the nurse, Stavro. Until the nurse comes, you are the nurse."

He ducks and rushes out through the door flaps. I glance around. Under the table, a stack of folded grey wool blankets. I kneel and grab one, shake it open, drape it over the woman, up to her fleshy chin above the scarved part of her brown hijab. Her head has tipped back but remains stable, presumably supported by her sturdy neck. She is motionless, unresponsive. *The victim is unresponsive.* Mentally I hear the phrase; I hear dispatchers radioing the phrase on TV medical dramas; I know the phrase means, as often as not, dead. Her waxen lips are parted, but when I lean close I hear no breathing. I see no rise and fall of her bosom under the wool blanket. Something leaps to mind: a young undertaker at a bar in Detroit telling me that our eyes, not used to seeing unbreathing chests, will always project slight motion into the chests of the dead. I do the math, get a double negative: if she were dead, I would see movement; I see none, she must be alive.

Her round, plump face is unwrinkled, though she must be in her fifties, maybe older. Expression not pained or stricken but serene, as if she is at home in her own bed, in dreamless sleep, somewhere back in Iraq before the wars. I hold my fingertips close to her lips. Is that a faint feathering of breath? I cup my hand over the pale band of brow showing under the edge of her hijab: no fever, no obvious chill. Could she be hypothermic and not chilled at the brow? I doubt it, but I'm not sure. I feel for her hand, fumbling under the edge of the blanket. This of course seems even more of a trespass than touching her face. I glance at the tent flaps, hoping to see the nurse push through, yet fearing I'll look like some pervert. And what if her family arrives? (Where *is* her family?) Some people, I've heard, feel titillated and licensed when left alone with an unconscious, helpless stranger. I feel scared shitless. I find her hand, soft but solid, larger than my own, and *warm*. Now I'm certain she can't be hypothermic. Hypothermic bodies siphon blood from the extremities to the core... don't they?

I lift her hand clear of the blanket and feel for the radial pulse under her sleeve. Her wrist is thick; I have to pinch hard. Still holding her hand, I crouch down beside the wheelchair. I locate the pulse, half-surprised to find it where I knew it should be. It seems steady, neither too heavy nor too faint. I check my watch. Hard to make out numbers in this light. Twenty-one beats in fifteen seconds? Still no response, but her signs seem OK.

There's nothing more for me to do except stay with her until the nurse returns. So I take up her hand again and simply hold it. "It's all right," I tell her. "Nurse will be here soon. You'll be all right." I assume that she can't hear me in her stupor and won't understand me if she can. I try to recall other moments in my life when I was thrust into a role of serious responsibility for which I felt unequipped. Maybe waking twenty years ago in a bed beside a wife and a four-hour-old daughter, the midwives gone home, the two of us improbably entrusted with this new life?

Over the next month, I and the other volunteers will repeatedly wake to find ourselves entirely unqualified but forced to act.

Greek was my mother's mother tongue, but not mine. Little by little now I am teaching myself, long after her death, as if the effort might span the chasm steadily widening between us. My limited grasp of Greek—overall the most difficult language I've tried to learn, including Japanese—is my lone qualification for volunteer work on Lesvos, besides a willingness to lend a hand however needed.

Her final decline and death of brain cancer, on a medical cot in my parents' living room, was backlit at times by news channel reruns of the recent World Trade Center attacks. The sound on the television was turned down or off. That footage, when she could see it—fleeting, peripheral splashes merging with her delirium—must have seemed even more dreamlike than it did to everyone else. I would sit beside her cot or help my father in the attached kitchen while the videos looped like trauma flashbacks in a single sleepless brain. America's response was going to be severe, anyone could see that, although it was hard to predict exactly what form it would take and impossible to foresee the eventual fallout.

Sooner or later something is going to jar you out of your slumber, if only for an hour. The question is, what are you going to do when it happens?

Sitting beside her after her death on Christmas Day, I let my head sag forward and come to rest on her impossibly still bosom, the way some people press their brows to the cool earth in prayer. We remained like that for an hour or more, the room dimming into dusk. I heard my father enter, flick on a light and fail to contain a violent, convulsive sob. Then, all but howling with grief, he fled the room.

The winds have died. Moonlight on the big-top shelters, the smaller tents and the prefab huts. The midnight camp might be a travelling circus in the respite between evening performance and morning tear-down. With Omiros and Asim I stand outside one of the shelters, its front flaps slightly open for air. The hum of space heaters and the sound of several hundred people's sleep-breathing fold into a drone as peaceful as collective chanting in a temple, mosque, or monastery.

Someone's loud, panicked blurting shatters the meditation. After a moment I ask, "What did he say? Do you know?"

Asim nods yes but doesn't translate. This is the first time I've seen him smoke. He exhales by coughing. His sunken eyes stare up at the moon. Omiros says, "I wish I can understand. My father left when I was young. I wish I can speak some Arabic."

Now a girl's piercing scream, followed by the hushing of a mother, aunt, or grandmother. Muted singing in a minor key—a lullaby?

West beyond the canteen and the highway a causeway of moonlight links Lesvos and the Turkish coast. That shimmering span, ten kilometres wide, more or less marks the crossing. When all is well and the sea is calm (tonight it wasn't), when desert people not qualified to steer a vessel manage to steer one (tonight they couldn't), when the overpacked dinghies don't flood or founder (tonight they did), when the disposable clip-on two-stroke engines don't seize up or run out of fuel because human traffickers versed in the basic maths of capitalism don't bother with oil or enough gas for more than a direct crossing in textbook conditions (tonight they weren't)—when all goes well, it's a two-hour journey.

From up here, the passage looks safe and easy, straight across waters moon-mapped as benignly as in a child's picture book.

"I know it," Asim stammers—"the one she's singing. My boat carries sugar and milk and tea. And we'll drink together at dawn."

Before wolflight

A WAVE OF NEW VOLUNTEERS, MAINLY YOUNG AND from northern Europe, has been arriving over the last twenty-four hours. Many are to be trained today. As for me, though I've worked a mere three shifts during my three days on the island, I'm now deemed to be trained—yet not experienced enough to train others. And since I've worked late at OXY these last two nights, Lindsay gives me a day off.

I wake in the dark in the shuttered room. Almost 10 a.m. Just outside the door, Elektra is shuffling her slippers and clicking her tongue. She's yearning to enter, evict me for the day and expunge any sign of my tenancy. She and her husband live right below. Although I'm trying to inhabit the room discreetly, she always knows whether I'm in or not. If I slip out to walk down to the bakery or the tiny grocery store, she flies in to reorganize and clean. These last

(

two days, I roughly made the bed before leaving for OXY. Returning, late, I found it remade according to rigorous, seemingly military specs. Weary, I could hardly force my way between the cold sheets, like the target of some college dorm prank. I'd closed a packet of Greek coffee with an elastic band; she'd replaced the band with a brown plastic clothes peg. I was keeping a pint bottle of ouzo in the freezer; she demoted it to the door of the little fridge. A bag of hazelnuts was removed from the fridge and placed on the table beside the clothes-pegged coffee, while a box of Greek cookies was taken from the table and secured in the fridge.

I decide to replace the brown clothes peg with a green one and see what happens.

I set out for Efthalou Beach, the third of the zones that the Captain's Kitchen volunteers take care of and the only one I have yet to see. The day is moody, grey and cool. I mean to hitch a ride from the edge of town, which is marked by the olive farmers' collective and a sanctuary for retired donkeys.

Fara is standing on tiptoe in faded high-tops at the sanctuary's stone fence. A cigarette wags between her lips as she encourages a donkey to take the apple she holds. Presumably too pampered, the animal only sniffs. From across the road comes the grinding of the oil press in the open work bay of the collective. Fara, in jeans and an untucked T-shirt, her hair unruly as a Gorgon's, looks more than ever like a romance heroine who has fled a privileged life to travel rough.

"OK, fuck it," she says hoarsely, dropping the apple at the donkey's feet and turning toward me. "Steve—is that right? Steve!" She hails me with a brusque familiarity, as if we serve on the same vessel and have bumped into each other on leave.

I explain where I'm headed.

"Don't bother, man. Nothing doing there today. You need to go to Skala. My ride should be here any time."

Skala Sykamineas is a village I've circled on the map, east up the coast beyond Efthalou. On its beach, I've heard, refugees have been landing all summer and fall. Other volunteer bodies, especially the anarchist group Antifa, are working there and have established a small transit camp.

Fara's ride pulls up: two men, maybe thirty years old— stubble beards, aviator shades, red fleece jumpers—stuffed into the front of a tiny Fiat.

"Come on, Steve. The Brothers K might need you. I'm going to be their translator."

Both named Kostas, both from Ioannou, two days' journey away across the Aegean and mainland Greece, they're doctors volunteering with the Hellenic Red Cross. The Fiat's floor crackles with chocolate wrappers and drink and food containers. Pillows and sleeping bags fill the hatch.

Like a motocross team they're driving us up into the mountains, the one at the wheel all but wrenching the shift out of its housing as he attacks steep grades and rockets out of cliffside curves. We crest hills like on a carnival ride that gives momentary vistas: the sea's border straits a few hundred metres down and, across the water, the naked grey mountains of Turkey.

My legs are jackknifed against the back of the driver's seat while beside me Fara, barely five feet tall, looks perfectly comfortable. She smokes, both Kostases smoke, I might as well smoke, so I do. Soon we're zippering down hairpin curves, the brake pads thumping and reeking. In contrast to this manic stunt driving, the doctors speak English with Old World decorum: "Now, we are about to arrive in the ancient fishing village of Skala Sykamineas..."

We brake and park. I unfold myself, climb free. After half an hour of automotive roaring and screeching, the silence and peace here seem profound.

Despite the economic crisis, and though we're near the epicentre of the refugee influx, the village resembles a set for a rom-com filmed on a Greek island. An old fisherman sits on a ladderback chair on the lip of the pier, mending his blood-orange nets with a large needle. Behind him a trio of boats, freshly painted in primary colours, bob at anchor. An ancient widow from central casting, maybe four foot eight hunched over, hobbles past, muttering to herself or at us.

Around the empty table on the pier an ensemble cast might be gathered—Judi Dench, Helen Mirren, Meryl Streep—sipping straw-yellow Moschofilero poured by a slim-hipped waiter with darkly ardent features. He is moodily silent but flashes a flirtatious leer as he bows and withdraws. The women are mystery writers, or maybe painters, trying to establish a retreat for women artists but meeting resistance from the lecherous and corrupt local mayor. Enter a handsomely greying Greek widower (initially remote, skeptical of their plans) who's returning from America to his childhood village in hopes of... etcetera.

No humanitarian crisis will impinge on the formula. The swarthy locals, like the singing slaves in *Gone with the Wind*—good sports one and all—will constitute a living greenscreen, that backdrop of picturesque penury that even intelligent romances deploy. Does the bourgeois fantasy-life always call for obliging menials, a supporting cast of massed extras to make the hero seem more preciously individual—in fact, more like a patrician?

What is the prince and princess's wedding without a mob of happy paupers to set it off?

I'm implicated in the pattern, like any worker in a crisis zone. Our efforts can make us feel not more connected to the people we're trying to help but more separate. Like patrons, not partners in the mission. You have to fight the tendency. You have to remind the ego (always keen to regard itself as special, always afraid of dissolution into the Many) that physical bodies all belong to one state without borders: the democracy of the dying animal. You can't help wishing someone would remind you of it every time you wake up for the rest of your life.

Kostas-the-driver checks his cellphone. "The intelligence says that boats will be arriving here this evening, perhaps after dark or at... *lykofos*. Wolflight?" He looks at me. "I forget the English word."

"Twilight?" I ask. "Dusk?"

"Dusk, exactly."

We walk west along a shoreline littered with empty water bottles, disposable diapers, a few shoes, a saturated pink parka, an infant soother, scores of red or orange life jackets. A fisherman and two German volunteers are struggling to haul an empty rubber raft up onto the beach. There are several more just beyond it. The rafts' no-name outboard engines are all still attached; apparently no one can be bothered to salvage them.

We roll up our pants and wade barefoot into the cool, pebbly shallows. The other Kostas lends me an extra pocket knife and we slash at the rafts' soft rubber floors, draining hundreds of litres of seawater. One by one, we manage to drag the rafts clear. Then we break them up as best we can and heap the remains onto cairns of wreckage and debris spread out along the beach—some dozen cairns and countless rafts. The plywood sheets used to cover the rubber bottoms we lean against the cairns. As I return his knife, Kostas tells me that the wood, once dry, will be used as "walling materials" in Skala's growing transit camp.

Before wolflight we go to Kima, "the Wave," a beach-front restaurant that Fara recalls from her previous stint here in the spring. As we enter, the owners and the aproned cook and middle-aged waitress all fall on her with cries and kisses and frenetic embraces, as if she's a daughter returning after many years abroad. For a moment all we can see of her is that froth of dark curls. She can't speak a word of Greek, and I'm reminded of how little such barriers matter to some people. As the Kima crowd yammers, she answers in English or pantomimes replies. A capacity for unmediated connection always makes me envious; I know that words, my stock-in-trade, cleave us more than connect us, and most dialogues are just overlapping soliloquies.

We're here for a brief rest, a drink and a snack, but this is Greece, so in no time a banquet breaks out. Kima is an unpretentious taverna, the tablecloth a sheet of butcher paper ripped from a roll, the cutlery weightless tin. The doctors know the menu—they too were here in Skala six months ago—and they order fried mullet, octopus both fried and grilled, stewed beets, *horta*, sliced white bread grilled in olive oil and herbs, and a light young table wine from Samos.

Two doctors on call, along with a translator and a new volunteer, sharing wine shortly before a refugee landing that could turn into an emergency… this drinking, however moderate, would flout protocol back home and seem an irresponsible indulgence. It doesn't here. Fara and the doctors are veterans and exude confidence and composure. And since Mediterraneans rarely drink to get drunk—to escape themselves and the soul-heft of Puritanical self-regulation—it seems natural for professionals dealing with serial crises to relax with a few glasses of wine.

As they pollute the air with cigarette smoke under a No Smoking sign ambered by years of nicotine, they touch on the logistical challenges of trying to integrate the many organizations now at work on Lesvos. There are Greek entities (the police, the coast guard, the civil authorities); volunteer groups like the Captain's Kitchen, some of which didn't exist even a month ago; political organizations such as Antifa; and, as of November, over *seventy* NGOs.

When I tell them I've heard that two volunteer groups ended up fighting over an arriving refugee boat last week, Fara reacts with coughing laughter. Kostas-the-driver frowns as he lights a cigarette.

"Fighting? You mean with hands, not words?"

"Arguing, anyway."

"Too many groups here, maybe. And yet, still not enough volunteers."

His sweeping gesture: the empty restaurant.

"It's like in Spain," I say, "1936. I was reading *Homage to Catalonia* last year—George Orwell's account of volunteering there?" (I pause as something occurs to me: could the residue of that immersive read have contributed to my decision to travel here?) Fara is nodding while the doctors look puzzled in the slightly grumpy way of high-status professionals used to being deemed authorities and delivering, not receiving, information. I mention the chaos behind the Republican lines during the Spanish Civil War: the elected Republican government, the Communist Party, anarchist bodies, and dozens of groups of foreign volunteers, speaking a babel of tongues, all fighting for the same cause but not always willing or able to coordinate. The Communists believing that, given the Soviet Union's support of the Republic, they are the leaders by association. The anarchists on principle uncooperative, fighting how and when they choose, yet fighting so effectively that their independence has to be tolerated. The volunteers likewise effective though at times undisciplined, temperamental, difficult to integrate into larger bodies for cultural and linguistic reasons... Remarkable that the Republic survived as long as it did and while facing unified opposition (why is it that the right always collaborates better than the left?) vanguarded by Spain's standing army with the direct support of Hitler and Mussolini.

Here is where the analogy breaks down. On Lesvos we're facing neither Franco's legions nor the Luftwaffe. Fara swats her hand through the smoke as if dismissing the whole notion: "Sure, yeah, the Spanish Civil War. Whatever. Those fuckers."

"Pardon?" says one of the doctors. They seem fascinated, smitten by Fara, though her slurry accent and slangy diction keep thwarting their efforts to hang on her words.

"So you disagree?" I ask her, refilling my wineglass.

"No, I'm totally with you, man."

"Pardon?" the other one says, scrunching his brow.

"All the NGOs... I don't know, man, I think they're just fuckers."

"You mean they pull rank on the rest of you?" I ask.

"What's that," she asks, "'pull rank'?"

"Try to boss everyone around."

"We have seen this here," the first doctor nods.

"It's weird," Fara says. "The volunteers are working for like nothing, so *they* should get more respect, right? But it's like the NGO people think 'cause they get the pay, they should get the respect. But maybe that's normal. So fuck normal."

It's just after 6 p.m. and already dark. No moon, no wind. Perfect conditions for an undetected crossing. Some refugees on the Turkish shore have been in touch with the Hellenic Red Cross by mobile phone: boats are on the way. A group of helpers is milling on the pebble beach.

Above the beach an arc light glares atop a spindly frame, as if for a news crew or a documentary shoot. But there are no journalists here. The Greek volunteers stand under the drastic light in red-crossed white plastic bibs, this regalia bearing an unfortunate resemblance to the tunics of the Crusaders who ravaged, raped, and occasionally cannibalized the Syrians of the Middle Ages and are still remembered there as terrorists.

The hum of anxious expectation is spiked by cries in Greek from the Red Cross volunteers. Under the hum runs the basso of generators from across the road that separates the beach from a row of soup sheds, tea huts, medical tents and slaphammer shelters—a little *favela* lit up by a string of light bulbs, their glow waning and surging. A few steadier lights shine above the Seventh-day Adventist medical hub: a white van to which a rough shelter, open at the front, has been annexed. I see a table stacked with supplies and a collapsible gurney.

The Kostases have donned their official bibs. Fara and I are following them through the crowd on the beach. At the waterline, three bibbed women stand signalling into the night with basic aluminum flashlights. No particular pattern—they're just blinking them on and off. The other volunteers seem uncertain where to stand. Some look terrified. Despite the arc light, sea and sky are a black berm, almost impenetrable. The flashlights stretch phantom arms a short way into the darkness. Nothing could possibly be out there.

We meet a volunteer Fara says she knows from last time and the two embrace and start chattering in Norwegian. I keep following the doctors. They mean to find me some of the packaged thermal blankets that the other volunteers are armed with, their pockets bulging, each packet the size of a soft-shell CD. But surely the doctors have better things to do. I'm a distraction. However much novices mean to help, they're always in the way, requiring the guidance and precious time of veterans and experts. So I tell them I'm going across the road to the medical hub to find blankets. "Yes, a good idea!" one of them says.

As I approach the van and shelter, a lanky man in a Seventh-day Adventist Medical Team hoodie and a Texas Rangers baseball cap greets me as if we've been acquainted for years but he's blanking on my name. "Hey there, you!" he says in a booming drawl. "Can I help you out someways? Looks like you're looking for something. That's a great chapeau!"

My misshapen felt hat, warm and rain-resistant, now looks more like an Aussie drover's working hat than the fedora it once was. I say I'm a volunteer and looking for thermal blankets.

"Sure, the space sheets! Got hundreds here. Come on under the shelter. I'm Gene, glad to meet you!" He clamps my hand. A lean, sun-shrivelled face and youthfully white teeth. He's speaking loudly, maybe to compete with the howl of the generator, though I sense it's his usual setting.

"I'm Steve."

"See what we built this from, Steve?"

"You mean the roof and walls?"

"Yep—they're the floors from all those boats! We salvaged them and built this baby. Got to make do around here, Steve. Here, take some of these sheets." He grabs two handfuls of packets from a box on the supply table. "When the boats show, just rip the plastic, shake the thing out, wrap it around the guy's shoulders and knot the corners at the throat, Little Red Riding Hood–style. Second knot here at the waist. Easy. Got it?"

More shouting from the beach and the tone is urgent, like people in a firing line preparing to repel invaders instead of receiving families in need. I hear a Greek word I know, *varka*, one of the first I learned as a child and one of the few I never forgot. *Boat*. I stuff the pockets of my jacket with thermal sheets. Gene plucks something out of a smaller box open at the top: rubber surgical gloves. "Here, Steve, put these on—you never know what you might be touching." I look at him and his pale eyes seem to retract and slide away slightly. "Blood, vomit, feces. Can't be too careful, Steve."

Stuffing the gloves into a pocket, I run back across the road. On the beach everyone stands frozen, peering into the compound darkness of sea and sky. Over the generators' drone a sound rises: the laboured chugging of a two-stroke engine. Then a higher sound that might be screaming. I can't see Fara or the doctors. The Red Cross women with their dollar-store flashlights are strobing the beams back and forth, searching the shallows and beckoning, "*Ela, ela'dho...!*" Faint voices echoing, responding. I edge toward the water, my sweating hands fumbling to tear the wrapping on two thermal blankets. I place an opened one in either pants pocket. More of that sourceless screaming.

Flashlight beams converge on a tight cluster of faces and torsos gliding in toward the beach. The raft itself is hardly visible: the top of the bow like a black rubber snout, the pontoon-like gunwales barely above water. Some of the passengers are sobbing, shrieking as if the sight of us terrifies them. My throat seizes up, my eyes sting.

In the shallows the bow scrapes upward and halts a few feet shy of the beach. Red Cross volunteers wade in, grip the hull handles and try to drag the raft up. It's way too heavy. A few soaked refugees are clambering onto the bow and leaping clear, as if the vessel is sinking instead of safely grounded. One kneels, pressing his brow to the beach. I can't tell if he's vomiting, praying, or both. Others are crawling or sliding over the sides into the shallows and wading in. Two Greek volunteers have climbed into the raft and are yelling something about needing help right now, "*Voithea—amesos!*"

A family emerges from the shallows on the port side. The heavily moustached father—in dripping parka and trousers, flip-flops on his feet—carries a small girl who looks mostly dry. The tall, sallow mother is shivering. The boy at her side has lost control of his jaw and clattering teeth. I shake open the silver thermal wrap and hold it up like a greeter at an airport with a sign. The mother nods. I wrap the sheet around the boy's wet, quaking shoulders and knot the corners at his throat—easily done because the material is so thin and pliable. Now I try to secure the lower corners at his waist and this is more awkward; I have to crouch and tie the knot just above his crotch. A smell of seawater and urine. I stand up, unpocket another wrap and turn toward the mother. Her hijab looks as wet as the rest of her layers. How will her husband feel about my knotting this thing at her waist? If we were better organized, we'd be working in male/female teams. As I hesitate, a male volunteer, fresh face, blond curls, German accent—"Here, we must be fast!"—steps in and expertly wraps her up. She ignores both of us, seems to be scolding her son for tugging at the knot at his chin.

Behind the family, two Red Cross volunteers are stretchering someone over the side of the raft, helped by a group of excited refugees. I get a newsreel flashback: a throng of mourners waving hands and chanting in Arabic as they run with an infant body on a bier. Beyond the raft some new object is entering the light-perimeter. My eyes refocus: a second raft.

A man staggers toward me like a drunk on a sidewalk, his eyes glazed and inflamed. I shake open a thermal wrap and enclose him, half expecting resistance. His body is racked by counter-rhythms, his sobbing, his shivering. One of the doctors appears and blurts something in Greek, then leads the man off.

The second raft is grating up onto the beach about fifty metres down. I run toward it and pass a man huddled under the arc light as if it's a heat lamp: trimmed beard, round spectacles, soaked trousers hugging bony legs. He's yelling into a cellphone, punctuating the Arabic with "OK, OK!" Somewhere a woman's voice calls, "Need a doctor here, *tora*! *Yiatros!*" Criss-crossing the havoc are scores of long, streaking shadows cast by the arc light and the swarming figures.

The second raft. A few of the fitter passengers are jumping off the bow into the shallows, peeling off life jackets and gathering around a Red Cross woman with a clipboard. These men look wet only from the knees down. As I run up, the woman asks me, "*Eisai ethelontis?* Volunteer?"

"*Nai, ethelontis.*"

"Take all this men up to the coffee… Wait, you speak Greek?"

"*Ligo*," I say: a little.

"Take them back for a hot drink," she says in Greek. "I think they're all right, but cold and hungry."

I turn to the men and say, "Please follow me." I wish I knew the Arabic phrase. Fara may be the only translator here and will be busy elsewhere. "This way." (Is that another flash of movement offshore? I don't look, I turn away, I stick to the task.)

The men follow closely, single file. We pass a tiny man in a longshoreman's toque, squatting on the stones, tilting his head back as he drains a plastic water bottle. One of the men behind me says, "Water, please."

"You speak English?" I ask.

"Water, please…"

I hurry them across the dirt road, past the Seventh-day Adventist medical hub. Gene—looking emaciated now instead of thin, as if he has somehow just lost twenty pounds—stands gaping at the beach, his limp hands dangling almost to his knees. Behind him, in that shantytown shelter, a doctor or medic is leaning over a figure stretched on the gurney.

"Gene!" I call. His evacuated eyes track toward me. "Gene? Do you know where I can find bottled water?"

"I have no answer to that question," he says in a hollow, zombified voice.

I veer right and the seven of us march up the road past tents and shacks while lost-looking people wander past us going the other way. Down on the beach, refugees are swarming out over the sides of a third dinghy. Ahead, others are queuing in front of a green-tarped field kitchen where a cauldron steams over a gas stove far too small for it. "We're here!" I call firmly, as if I've known all along where we were going. We join the queue. After some moments I give two of the men, now shivering, my last thermal blankets, then head back toward the medical van for more. I'm trotting, almost running, so adrenalized I couldn't walk if I tried.

The doctor still attends to his unmoving patient. Gene is absent, perhaps being treated for his parasympathetic shock, or whatever it was. No more thermal wraps on the supply table. I'm stuffing the unused rubber gloves back into the box when he steps down out of the van, ducking his ballcapped head under the steel lintel. He's pale but grins broadly as he sees me. "Steve!" Another spirited Texas welcome, as if our brief, Beckettian last exchange never happened.

For a couple of hours we remained on the beach, awaiting two other rafts that had embarked with the first three. I grew steadily more worried; the doctors and Fara reassured me that vessels that set out together rarely arrived together. The missing ones, if not rescued by the coast guard, would have landed elsewhere to the west after drifting, mis-steering, or simply aiming for other beacons on other beaches.

"But could they have sunk?" I asked.

"In such conditions, no," said one of the doctors. "In such conditions, the worst possible thing is... well, really very bad. Last month, several boats drifted past the final, the final... *pos to lene, akrotiri?*"

"Cape," the other said heavily.

"The final cape of Lesvos. They were seen a far distance out, but never found. One day, we may discover boats on one of the deserted islands."

"And bodies, I'm afraid," said the other. "Bones."

"But many boats have been arriving tonight at Efthalou. The other two are probably among them. We will be certain later."

Nine p.m.: a number of refugees are being treated for shock or hypothermia inside the medical van and the Red Cross tent. The other two hundred or so, Afghans as well as Syrians, have been bused half an hour over the mountains to OXY. A few Red Cross sentinels remain on the beach, drinking tea around a luridly yellow, obviously toxic bonfire of life jackets, while most of us retreat to a restaurant charmingly called "I zoi en tafos"—Life in the Grave. Inside, a long-dead mulberry tree as thick as a baobab erupts out of the flagstone floor and passes through an opening in the roof. The seal around it doesn't keep the rain from trickling down the lacquered bark into the restaurant.

Beside this magnificent corpse, a plaque. Author Stratis Myrivilis was born in Skala Sykamineas in 1890 and wrote his best-known novel (the source of the restaurant's name, I see now) at a café table under the boughs of this tree after serving in the Greek army's campaign in Turkey in 1922. The plaque doesn't mention that after the Greek defeat, countless boatloads of Asian Greek civilians had to flee with him and the army across the straits to Lesvos—the very vector that current refugees are following almost a century later.

I've known about that earlier exodus, or call it ethnic cleansing, for years. Yet it was only a few nights ago on the ferry, reading about Lesvos, that I learned those Greek refugees had followed this same escape route. (Of course they had; Lesvos is the closest main island to Turkey.) Even more oddly, only now does it strike me that along with those refugees must have come relations of my own: some with the name Afaganis, "from Afghanistan," and some bearing my grandmother's surname, Smyrlis, "of Smyrna," a city across the straits and now called Izmir—the chief staging point for the current wave of human traffickers and asylum seekers.

I say "oddly," but don't we always look past the obvious—those facts and stories we've breathed in from infancy? And isn't it often the things we overlook, forget or bury that catalyze our decisions, as they constellate our dreams?

So here I stand in Life in the Grave. A hanging fireplace, packed bodies, the warm smoke of cigarettes and pipes... the place is snug and noisy. Fara and her friend are catching up at a small table, two petite, chain-smoking women whose jug of beer looks enormous between them. I sit down with the doctors and two older Antifa volunteers. These women are friendly at first but steadily less so; once it's clear that my Greek is too flimsy for serious conversation, we default to English, and the women can't manage as well as the doctors. As the beer and the shots of *raki* relax them while also making them less patient—more intent on voicing vital matters efficiently and clearly—they start snapping off sentences and then whole thoughts in Greek. Soon they quit speaking English altogether. As the doctors too switch over, their formality vanishes and I realize that what I saw before as calm, courtly deliberation was simply the effect of having to overthink every phrase.

The moment all four settle into Greek, talking politics, how Fascism is revanchist all over Europe, I become a ghost. Could their now-exclusive, quadrilateral focus signal the start of an impromptu double date? But the doctors don't look interested that way. Nor do the older women. When intellectually engaged Europeans talk politics, it's always more than a mere proxy for emotions or desires. One of the women—a pinched chain-smoker given to indignant grins and derisive laughter, especially after references to the Greek government and the NGOs—scowls as she notices me trying to follow. I feel a bit hurt, but I get it. I've been in their position, humouring a non-fluent outsider while eager to skip ahead to the night's freer, wittier, creatively collaborative phase, jazz artists indulgently jamming with a student. I walk to the bar past that fabled tree still weeping with rain and fetch another pint, then find a corner table and dig out my pen and lined journal—all but empty, no chance to write a word until now—and begin scribbling notes.

Disposition is destiny. Its data points—the experiences you select, save and revisit, and that somebody else might have instantly deleted—form a living archive, the reference library of your character.

I'm a few days into my teen years. It's August 1974, hot in Toronto but hotter in every sense in the eastern Mediterranean. On Cyprus, the UN has brokered a fragile truce and interposed a Green Line between the invading Turkish army and the outnumbered Greek Cypriots. It's rumoured that the military regime in Athens has been flying Greek commandos into Cyprus to help the losing side. At any moment a larger war might break out between Greece and Turkey. A river of refugees, both Greek and Turkish Cypriot, is flowing in two directions across the Green Line. Ethnic cleansing: a term not yet in use in 1974.

I'm sitting at the kitchen table reading a book while my mother, Lambrini George Stephanopoulos, scrapes and scrubs every dish in the sink before racking it in the dishwasher, a practice whose seeming redundancy fills my teenaged soul with annoyance. Still, on the whole she and I get along well and I like being in the same room with her if I'm reading, as I usually am. The radio is tuned to a Toronto Greek station, probably on the Danforth. Its Hellenic uproar—songs! news! weather! ads!—is no impediment to concentration, since I understand none of it.

My English-Canadian father enters the kitchen. For some reason my mother leaves. The lugubrious song on the radio ends and a male voice starts declaiming in staccato Greek with a slight, ominous reverb effect. My father glances at the clock—6 p.m.—then tilts his head, biting his lower lip, trying to follow the speaker's ranting. He knows just a little Greek.

"What's going on?" I ask.

He cranks the radio higher. That terrifying voice shakes the room. "Lambie," he calls, "come back! I think Greece and Turkey have gone to war!"

She runs into the kitchen, stops, regards the radio for a moment through her cat-eye glasses. "It's a carpet sale on the Danforth," she says.

On the pier at Petra

THE EMBLEM OF TODAY'S EMERGENCY IS A WIRY LIT-tle cop in a SWAT officer's black forage cap, the brim pulled low over a face that is little more than mirrored sunglasses and a surgical mask. He stands on the pier in full crotch-display, riot boots planted far apart, tactical knee pads, holster bulging with a sleek Glock. Hands behind his back, he's motionless as a mannequin, as if the bankrupt authorities are now propping effigies wherever security is required.

Half an hour ago I was standing in the food hut at OXY, part of a four-person assembly line mass-producing processed-cheese-on-white sandwiches. I was on mayonnaise detail. From the little amp outside the bus ticket kiosk, the bleating of R & B electronica. Entering the hut, Lindsay softly announced that the coast guard was about to land a hundred refugees in Petra and she needed help.

As I followed her outside, she relit her hand-rolled cigarette and explained that a large, crowded dinghy had capsized on the northern side of the straits. The Turkish navy—always ready to let nature take its course—had shown no inclination to get involved, so a Greek coast guard vessel had crossed into Turkish waters to help the refugees. The ship, the coast guard's largest, was now ferrying these people to the deepwater pier at Petra, since Mithymna harbour was too shallow. Lindsay needed me and Eva, a Danish volunteer, to go down to Petra with a hundred thermal blankets. Lindsay would join us soon but first had to deal with another problem (she took a long, famished drag) here at OXY.

Eva is waiting for me astride a motor scooter on the edge of the highway. Unlike the other student volunteers she is mostly silent, contained, like a woman who has just emerged from an extended meditation retreat. Yet here she is now, revving the scooter's ill-tuned little engine with zest, beaming at the marvellous novelty of each roar.

I climb on the back and we surge away down the long hill toward Petra—a few minutes south of OXY and a thousand feet below. A sunny December afternoon, almost warm. Opening ahead and to the west are luminous frescoes of Petra's sparkling bay and, behind it, olive-tree terraces climbing the mountains to the wild upper slopes. The wind smells of sun-hot oregano, sage, pine resin. It's sweet to feel the wind in my hair—in Greece helmets are an exception, not the rule—but as Eva's long hair keeps lashing my face and the scooter weaves as if entering a speed wobble, I'd be glad for a helmet. She is probably just a few years older than my daughter, whom I taught to drive just two years ago. I holler, "You haven't driven one of these before, have you?"

"What…? Never! Nor a car. But many bicycles."

At the bottom of the hill we lean into a curve and Eva, uncertain of our route, slows to a tottery crawl. "I think *there*," I yell over a suddenly mounting roar. Our own puny engine? As she turns right off the highway, a car missiles past on the right side, the inside, close enough to kick— streak of burnt orange, slipstream blast, dopplering horn. She brakes and swerves leftward, a reflex manoeuvre deftly executed, either through inborn talent or beginner's luck. We come to a stop, my pulse smacking up against my palate. She draws a deep breath and releases it as hearty laughter. "Oh, wow!" she says.

The welcome party awaiting the refugees includes representatives from two NGOs and several volunteer groups; three cops, including that dystopic scarecrow in the sunglasses and pandemic mask; and an unaffiliated Scottish frogman named Hamish, who stands apart grimly smoking in a wetsuit and flippers.

The *Nike*, at first hidden behind a mole of boulders on the north side of the pier, now sweeps into view. It reverses into position slowly, engines throbbing. High on its sunlit deck a crowd of refugees huddles against the navy-grey bridge. A handrailed gangplank slides down off the deck and clunks onto the pier. Two officers march down it. The refugees rise and file behind them. No one is offering them help, nor do they need it. Again, even the older folks and children move swiftly, calmly and in good order, as if this situation is routine: disembarkation under guard from an armed foreign vessel after an emergency sea rescue.

The usual mayhem of good intentions and cross pur-
poses follows as different volunteer groups push in among
the refugees, Afghans as well as Syrians today. The NGO
wonks—in plastic vests branded with acronyms, gripping
their clipboards like lecterns—distract the volunteers with
redundant commands. *That one there needs a space blanket! I
think this kid is dehydrated—bring water!* The frogman stands
to one side, slouching in his wetsuit, seemingly dejected
that no one has yet fallen off the pier.

Eva is trying to wrap a young woman in a thermal
sheet. The woman curtly refuses, produces a tiny compact
and proceeds to examine her grey, strained, pretty face. A
young Afghan with a wide, bronze-burned face—he could
pass for Tibetan—stands on tiptoe, searching the crowd.
Seawater puddles on the asphalt around his high-top sneakers. I stare at his sweatshirt, where an approximation of a
certain professional hockey team's emblem is emblazoned
with the words TORONTO KAPLE LEAFS and, below it, in
a smaller font, BREATHE FRELIY. Another young man
jabbers into his clamshell phone, smiling while his teeth
chatter and whole frame shudders. He ignores me while I
wrap a thermal blanket around his shoulders and, as unob-
trusively as possible, knot it under his wagging chin.

Someone calls me almost inaudibly. I turn around:
Lindsay. She asks for an update. I speak and as she listens,
head bowed, she rolls a cigarette with her left hand. No
other part of her moves. Weariness is limiting any exertion
to that one hand, those nervous, nimble fingers. If she didn't
smoke, her nails would be bitten raw. Her stillness, her
voice's softness... *is* she depressed after her months here
or just carefully containing herself in order to withstand it?

She lights up and inhales like a desert wanderer sucking water through a straw.

Two little Fiats snarl onto the pier and screech to a stop. Several people leap out—not a riot squad, not customs officers, but three squat, spry old women and a bearded giant (how did that car contain him?) with a huge head of black curls. Yammering in Greek they throw open the hatches and lift out cardboard boxes overflowing with clothes. The man is the local priest, Lindsay tells me, the women are parishioners who collect clothing for the refugees and also distribute things donated from abroad. As the priest bellows something, he and the fit old women, one in a widow's dress and with blue-rinsed hair, hustle away with their boxes.

The faceless cop continues to stand frozen at the base of the pier. Two buses pull in behind him, but it will be some time before anyone can board them. As in Mithymna harbour my first night, the refugees are deemed to be under arrest until registered, and now there is registration trouble.

Lindsay and I huddle with the International Crisis Relief rep—an aloof, officious woman from Ottawa—and the *Nike*'s short, hawk-faced captain, who wears a watch cap and is gauntly unshaven. Not getting much sleep these days. The ICR rep, tapping her clipboard with the back of her pen, states that Lindsay was to bring the registration forms. Lindsay murmurs that just now at OXY an ICR person told her *they* would supply the forms and, if they didn't, the Greek coast guard would have some. We all look down at the captain. "*Ochi!*" he cries, *no!*, closing his eyes and tossing up his hands as if to say, *Has the coast guard not done enough for one day?*

"Oh, no," Lindsay says. "Fuck, we need to get these people sheltered. I'll go to the police station for more forms."

"More forms? We don't have *any* forms!" the ICR rep corrects her.

"*Sas eucharisto*," the captain thanks Lindsay, ignoring the other woman—and as Lindsay rolls a smoke for the road he offers her a Marlboro from his pack.

I watch her peel away in the Captain's Kitchen Mini. Minutes later I hear and see the car buzzing up the long grade toward OXY and Mithymna. But fetching any forms now, with shops and offices shuttering for lunch and the siesta, might take longer than we hope.

Refugees are churning through the boxes of clothing. Against the concrete wall below the mole on the north side, women have improvised changing tents by holding up thermal blankets, behind which other women are trying things on. They must be tempted to squat and urinate in those shelters; for whatever reason, they're not being allowed to use the public toilets now hidden behind the buses at the foot of the pier. I do the math, based on what I've learned this past week. At least two hours from their camp in the Turkish forest to the shore and the boats. An hour or two at sea until the sinking in mid-channel. A half-hour on the deck of the *Nike*. An hour and counting here on the pier.

At least five hours already. Yet even the children and the older folks continue to look serene, almost cheerful. A young Afghan man calls out to his friends as he holds up the new yellow hoodie he just pulled from one of the boxes.

The low winter sun tracks lower to the west. The day, mercifully mild until now, cools as we wait for Lindsay and the forms. Maybe something has gone wrong. By 3 p.m. the refugees are beginning to droop. Some families sit down, clumped close together, against the still-sunny seawall, although most of the hundred remain standing. Anyone kept waiting for hours becomes superstitious: To sit down is to send a signal of resignation or defeat. To stand and look ready is to conjure, or compel, a swifter outcome. Discouragingly, the drivers of the two buses now kill the engines. A faint sigh eddies through the crowd. A woman with a toddler who wears a wolf-face toque looks at me questioningly. I splay my hands with a helpless half smile. The priest and the old women pack up the remaining clothes, ease shut the car hatches and drive away, slower now, as if departing a funeral.

The self-propelled clipboard appears beside me, her voice nasal with annoyance. "Do we have an ETA on those registration forms?" I shake my head. "Right," she exhales, as if worn down by the indignity of working with untrained personnel and in such ad hoc conditions. Wondering how she regards OXY, I draw her out by mentioning Omiros's and Lindsay's latest improvements: a children's play area and space heaters for the big tents. After a moment she says, "We have six people on the ground at OXY every day." I expect her to elaborate and so I wait, nodding reasonably, thus missing my chance to point out that in fact her people at OXY do little more on the ground than stand around on it. Add this lapse to the ledger of truths undelivered over the years because I was struggling to force a positive construction on somebody's words—to somehow see the best in them.

Lindsay arrives at last, leaping out of the car and running toward us, flustered, sweating, apologetic.

"So, we have the correct forms now?" the ICR rep says, lips barely moving.

"Yes! And bagged lunches, from OXY!"

"Great," I say, flashing a glance at the rep; you can always trust stiffly clerical types to opt for "correct" when "right" would do. Lindsay ignores the jab. Maybe like me she prefers to pick her fights and keep them few? More likely she believes this is no time to gratify her feelings by responding.

She stations me in front of the buses—engines again idling, spewing fumes—with a heavy-duty garbage sack stuffed with bagged lunches and bottled water. The ICR rep stands at the open door of the bus, conferring with the driver, who squats above her on the top step fingering his worry beads. Newly registered refugees straggle toward us from the pier and I start handing out lunches and water.

The rep walks toward me, frowning consequentially at her clipboard.

"You can distribute the food but they can't eat it."

"What?"

"The drivers don't want them eating on the coaches."

"Jesus... Can they drink their water, at least?"

"I wasn't given that information." Fraught pause. "I think maybe they shouldn't... shouldn't bother. The bus toilets are locked."

"But it's been hours already!" I say, revising my addition (OXY is full up and it's over an hour down to Moria, where they'll have to go through a second, more official, round of registration, hence another couple of hours). "Eight or nine hours total," I say. "No toilet."

She nods, sliding her sunglasses up the bridge of her nose. The sinews tighten in her thin neck. She wishes

I hadn't spelled things out. When natural alphas don a uniform they become more confidently bossy. When less forceful, passive people like her suit up, they can turn peevish, prickly, always anticipating challenges to an authority they're never sure of and perhaps don't even want.

It strikes me that she too might be exhausted, quietly panicking.

"Let's ask again if they'll let them use the public toilets," I say.

"I *tried* that, of course—I care about these people too!"

The queue is starting to back up. I resume handing out the bags and bottles while she instructs the mystified refugees, wagging a chiding finger as if they're grade schoolers boarding an orange bus: "Must—not—eat—on—the bus! No—toilet—on—the bus...!"

Twenty steps away the waxwork cop stands watching. He has removed his sunglasses but the low brim of his cap keeps his eyes hidden. His shoulders stoop now; he too must be getting tired; suddenly he seems almost approachable. "So, what do you think of all this?" I call in Greek. He raises a palm white as a dandy's glove—a signal I might read as anything from a greeting, to an assurance that all is well, to a silent order: *Do not address me!* The ICR rep prattles on in her toddler talk and for the first time I feel truly uneasy in my role here—a barely helpful neophyte stuck between that cartoon of weaponized authority and this patronizing functionary.

Overtaken by the night

THE NEXT DAY BREAKS CLEAR AND WARM AGAIN. I'M slated for the 3 till 11 p.m. shift at OXY, so for an hour this morning I sit in the sun on the concrete balcony of the guest house with a loaf of still-warm bread, pistachios, a pomegranate, and a succession of beautifully bitter Greek coffees prepared over my room's one-flame propane burner. The grind is fine as climber's chalk, russet and sweet-smelling as if cut with cocoa. Spoon some into a *briki* with water, heat it, and just when the mixture boils up and over, pour into a small cup.

On reaching for the packet this morning, I saw that Elektra had again refastened it with the brown clothes peg I've been daily, wryly replacing with a green one—but this time she has also hidden or taken away the green peg.

A fine-print dictionary and reading glasses lie on the table by my cup as I lip-read my way through *Ta Nea*, a left-leaning Greek newspaper, to follow news of the crisis while also working on my Greek. (Two days ago I bought a right-wing tabloid—simpler diction, shorter articles, but a struggle to read anyway.) My truant brain keeps skipping class, browsing the world beyond the page for diversions: the view over terracotta-tile rooftops down to Petra Bay and westward to the final cape of Lesvos, the translucent ruby of a pomegranate seed fallen on the white plastic table. Greece with its sun and heat and food and drink and stripped-down beauty excels at these seductions and sedations, luring the serious and the studious back down into the body and—continuing along that sensual vector—out into the world.

A slow, heavy tread on the concrete stairs connecting the porch to street level. I expect to see Elektra's husband trudge into view. Instead a young soldier appears: garnet beret, camouflage fatigues, the sleeves rolled up over forearms thick as hawsers, the pants tucked into combat boots. His brow is crimped in a scowl as if he just humped up ten storeys. For a moment I wonder if I'm in trouble of some kind; then I recall that Elektra's son is in the army and home on leave.

"This journal you read," he says in English. "You can really read it?"

"*Me dyskolia*," I say, putting it down over the pomegranate seed. *With difficulty.*

"You are Steven," he says in English. "I am Adonis."

I stand and take his offered hand. The grip is surprising—utterly lax. He is tightening his smooth jaw instead.

His narrowed eyes dubiously inspect me, as if he has already caught me in a lie.

"Would you like a coffee?" I ask in Greek.

"My mother makes good Greek coffee," he says in English.

"It is good. I've been down there to check email and I've had some." (I don't mention how his mother constantly looms behind me, bringing more coffee, a cookie, a cigarette, obviously monitoring the screen over my shoulder.)

He says, "You tell her that you have no smartphone for mail."

"I did. I mean, I don't."

He smirks. "Yet you are here for a month?"

"Yes."

"Why do you come?"

This exchange might feel less like an interrogation if we sat down, but what is the etiquette? Do I offer him one of these plastic chairs—his own parents' chairs, *his* chairs? He leans back against the low wall of the porch and folds his arms over his chest. The sunned and muscled forearms are hairless as a girl's.

"I kept hearing about what was happening," I say. "I decided to come and help."

A broad, bitter smile. He looks down at his boots. They're buffed so clear he can probably see his reflection in the toecaps. "Others, they tell me this same thing. But you are older than they. You have no life, no family?"

I explain my circumstances. I'm a writer, I live simply, I was between drafts of a book. My daughter is grown up. I had this opportunity—this luxury.

I sense he doesn't know this last word and reach for the dictionary.

"And your wife?"

"It was a good time for a break." I pause. "Some time apart."

"For me, it's hard to believe—coming so far to help strangers. This is not how people are. Always there is some other reason."

I set the dictionary down. "I guess that's often true."

"Always true."

"But we don't always know what the reason is." I'm not going to bring up my ethnic connection; Greek nationalists scoff at rootless diasporics like me. "I know I wanted to see what was going on here and report back."

"So, you are a reporter—a journalist!"

"Not exactly."

"This journal you read"—his forearms flex but stay locked, his hands untypically static for a Greek voicing an opinion—"it is always full of left-wing lies."

"What about *Vradyni*?" I ask, naming the major right-wing paper, which of course is anti-Muslim, anti-refugee.

"And these students—why they come here? Why not they stay in their own countries and help the, the—their *sympatriotes*? No one needs help in your rich countries?"

"Maybe more need it there."

"But they come here, the students! For the sun and the wine, Germans and Danish on a school leave."

I could docket exceptions: Iphigenia, once a girl goatherd here on the island, now married to a Greek American in Connecticut and returning, she says, to help her people;

Cyrus, a young Iranian with a full beard and a roguishly tilted porkpie hat, who studies law in Seattle and is here as a Farsi interpreter; Ratko, a hulking, growling Serb in hot water of some kind back home, got up like a Russian gangster in a black toque and sweatsuit; Shayn and Astrid, a petite couple of great physical and spiritual beauty, he South Asian with an Aussie accent, cargo shorts in all weathers and minimalist trainers like simian feet that prompt gawking and giggling among the usually stolid refugees, she the graduate of a Pippy Longstocking upbringing, looking calm, fit and perfectly fresh after an overnight shift. Then the exception who proves the rule: a pale, pretty young American who hangs out with our crew but self-identifies as an "independent." Did she arrive with good intentions and then, faced with dawn and graveyard shifts, reconsider? See her at the Captain's Kitchen for drinks and a Greek salad, iPad in hand, see her hydrating in cafés, see her strolling the lanes with a selfie stick or floating past in a car's passenger seat: spa-day smile and First Lady wave.

"But this is a crisis," I tell Adonis. "Help is needed here urgently, right? When those students go home, maybe..."

"And these migrants! Why not they stay in their own countries and fight the terrorists? They come here for the money and the jobs. Not here, no—here there is nothing! I mean to Germany. Here now, even the tourists will not come. Only you volunteers come and you will not stay long."

As if the light is now too much, I put on my sunglasses. I tell him it moves me to see people that age (his age, in fact) acting in service to something, not just existing automatically, apolitically, narcissistically. "You know what I mean?"

"Of course I know! All these words, their roots are Greek."

Reactionary young soldiers are not supposed to care about such things, but in Greece the Tinkertoy stereotypes of my world are demolished daily.

"Anyway," he says, "they are rich, the young ones here."

"I think some are broke, actually. I mean poor. And I'm not rich."

Another caustic smile. "If you are not rich, how could you be here?" He unlocks his arms and slides a pack of cigarettes from his breast pocket, finds it empty, drops it on *Ta Nea*. He looks to one side as if searching for an English word, then speaks quietly, almost sheepishly. "Maybe I am rude. My parents always tell me this—Adoni, you are too aggressive. But listen!" His hands, now freed, chop at the air. "In Greece some of us still have jobs, we work hard, and still we are not paid! I am not paid in over two months."

No way to respond but with unfeigned surprise and a sympathetic head shake. I've heard that the coast guard and the cops have not been paid in weeks, but the army too, here on the front line, facing Erdogan's Turkey?

"Enough," he says. "I will leave you quietly. My mother expects me."

As he turns toward the stairs I say, "I hope your leave—your *adeia*?—goes well."

"Yes, my *adeia*. And I hope you enjoy your holiday."

At 2 p.m. I head for the camp. Today I shun the street and jigsaw my way downward through limestone alleys and stairways in the deep breathless silence of siesta. I pass an orange tree, its sagging fruit somehow forgotten in spite of the island's current woes and the presence of thousands of hungry people.

I reach the highway at the edge of town, stick out my thumb and walk backward. I was expecting at least a few buses to pass, shuttling new arrivals from Skala or Efthalou Beach, but the road too is silent, as if the whole crisis has ended overnight or shifted elsewhere. Down from the mountain comes the ancient music of autumn on the Aegean isles—the tinkling melody of goat bells, the backbeat of sticks slapped against branches to bring down the olives.

New weather is rolling out of the north, a vast awning of cloud. By the time I reach OXY, still on foot, the front overtakes me. The temperature troughs. Warning shots of rain pitter down, then the sky looses an icy barrage. Cruel timing; the packed buses I had expected to see out on the road are now appearing and pulling in. In the lower parking lot, other buses wait to ferry the refugees on to Mordor, as volunteers who have been to Moria now call the place.

Rain drills down like shrapnel. The sky darkening hours early, I recall a verb I stumbled on in the dictionary this morning: *nyhtonomai*, "to be overtaken by the night."

I'm slated for bus-boarding duty but that won't start until the new arrivals are clothed and fed, so Lindsay asks me to pitch in for now at the men's clothing tent. In front of it, the queue is herniating into a mob as the rain intensifies, pitting and rilling the dirt. The tent's fussy foremen, Dieter and Oskar, won't arrive until the night shift starts at eleven, so again I find myself teamed with the saintly Klaus along with Larry Silver, an American with big square glasses, a brushy grey moustache and a French painter's beret. He's the oldest volunteer in the group, an ex–investment banker whose politics have tipped leftward since retirement. From his current home in Provence he has travelled here in a battered Westphalia camper van along with his companion, a shy, subdued bloodhound named Chet. In manner, Larry veers from affably avuncular—he has the warm, folksy baritone of a public radio talk-show host—to peevish. His testiness comes in spasms, as if he's suffering from a physical pain or fatigue he can't always manage. He's a Bernie Sanders supporter and at times seems hopeful about Sanders's chances, though yesterday he grumbled with a certainty I saw no reason to doubt, "Hillary Rodham Clinton will be the next president of the United States."

As for Klaus, I've learned that his volunteering is the latest stage in a journey he calls a Peace Trek. For three years he has been walking around Europe, Africa, and especially Asia. No possessions, no money. Every evening he will knock on the door of a stranger and ask for food and shelter. In this way he has traversed China, Tibet, Pakistan, Iran, Afghanistan, Iraq, Syria, the Occupied Territories, Israel, Gaza... And was it not hard for him to get across borders? "*Ja*, sure, sometimes they arrest me, so I have a warm night in jail." He is thin—as befits a mendicant with a wicker begging bowl—yet not emaciated. Folks everywhere have been generous. "A door will shut in your nose sometimes, *ja*, but not often do you go without supper and shelter." In his sandals and white drawstring pants he always treads softly, thoughtfully, as if considerate even of pavement, gravel, dirt. Naturally he walks out to OXY every day and—sometimes overtaken by the night—back into town again. Around fifty, balding, he has a freckled pink scalp and weather-worn features. His muted voice is self-effacing, yet there's a puckish spark in his blue eyes as he makes shrewd, amused observations.

A few nights ago, when I helped here briefly, the refugees were too cold and desperate to form a patient line. Today it's the rainstorm pushing them in—seeking shelter as much as clothing. We need to do this fast. For a few minutes Klaus and Larry and I hold our own, the two men calling requests back to me—*pants, large… coat, small boy's… shoes, size eight*—while I scramble, ducking the two hanging bulbs in the dully lit tent, locating stuff. Dieter and Oskar must have been here this morning; the tent's contents have been ferociously curated; the good order is helping me keep up.

But every time I return with something, the front of the crowd has splayed wider and is pressing in harder. A young man edges sidewise around the barrier of the tables, speaking in Arabic as he points at his shoes and lifts his foot. The shoe flaps open like a puppet's mouth. Larry orders him back. The man shrugs, tries again to explain. Two men are slipping in around the other side. Now a beefy man with a broad, aggressive smile—he is used to ordering, not asking—shoves to the front. None of the men he has bumped aside protest. I signal to the other two who are trying to slip in: please wait. They pause and nod, but as I hustle back toward the clothing bins I see them, peripherally, pushing in again. "Get the hell out of here!" Larry snaps, the first angry command I've heard any volunteer issue.

The big man is suddenly next to me at the back of the tent: carnivorous grin, black eyes flashing as he gestures toward a pair of oxblood brogues. His own shoes look scuffed but solid. I point back at the queue: "Please go wait in line." He snatches the brogues and walks off, meanwhile raising his free hand like a stop sign, ordering the other men back. For a moment they retreat. Then they resume pushing in. Within minutes the tent is steaming with wet, shivering men rifling through bins and boxes. Their clouding breaths are rank with the ketones of hunger. Klaus, Larry and I have been demoted to mere observers trying to ensure that no one grabs more than one of anything.

"Larry, this guy here"—I nod toward a haggard adolescent, who's pointing at his shredded trainers—"he still doesn't have any shoes."

"He checked all the shoes," Larry snarls. "He just didn't like the style."

But Larry's mood doesn't affect his work ethic, and when the rush finally dies off he once more radiates fatherly goodwill toward everyone, refugees and volunteers alike. Does he mind if I go help out at the buses now? "Sure thing, Steve. You too, Klaus. We got a lot of folks into nice dry stuff, huh? I can hold the fort here on my own."

I put on my fedora and splash past the two UNHCR tents, full of people sitting, eating a hot meal, waiting for their turn to board a bus. Kanella's barking, muffled by the pelting rain, comes from inside the canteen hut where she has to stay at busy times. I join the other volunteers at the bus-boarding zone: five roped-off lanes sloping down to the lower parking lot, where a fleet of buses sit idling. The ropes, slung from rebar stakes pounded into the dirt, are trimmed with ribbons and parti-coloured scraps like prayer flags. These could be ticket lanes at an indie music festival.

On a wooden post at the head of each lane hangs a board painted with a symbol: red heart, black diamond, green flower, blue lemniscate, yellow circle (on which someone has drawn a happy face). Refugees travelling together receive chits marked with one of the symbols and line up accordingly, so that family and village units, as well as ethnic and linguistic groups, stay unified. Today I'll be collecting the chits, counting out sixty—one busload, minus small children, who can sit on their parents' laps—then admitting the group to a boarding lane closed off at the lower end by another volunteer.

Refugees are emerging out of the tents into the rain. A Dutch film crew is recording everything for a news documentary, the cameraman hunched under a streaming black poncho like a Victorian photographer under a cape. From the base of the lane, the shift foreman, an MFA student from Baltimore named Jaquon, yells something I can't quite hear over the music now thumping out—the Clash, *London Calling*—but I think he said *Two minutes*.

The buses are backing into position. I turn to face the refugees—they're getting soaked all over again—and raise two fingers. "Two minutes!" A man of about twenty-five stands at the front, a step away. His blue eyes bulge at me. His red hair, receding at the temples, is plastered to his skull. Trimmed goatee, skin sunburned pink. Among the darker, black-haired Syrians he looks almost albino. One of the men says something to him and he—keeping his eyes on my face—replies in Arabic. Then to me, in barely accented English: "Will there be enough buses?"

"I can't say for sure"—I have to raise my voice over the Clash—"but I hope so. We hope so."

"Why are you not allowed to say? This is some secret?"

"No, I mean I'm not sure."

"You are not sure." He stares, blinking rain out of his eyes. It's pummelling down, dripping off the end of his nose, sluicing in streams off my hat brim. My jacket is damp and heavy. The people behind him look back and forth between us.

"You're the first fluent English speaker I've met so far," I say.

"Yes, I am acting as translator on our journey."

"I've wanted to ask... I hope you don't mind... the crossing... what was it like?"

A blank look—then he nods. "Good luck was with us. The water was only to our knees. I was scooping with a pail. But some were too afraid to do anything."

"You weren't afraid?"

"Something gave me strength," he says, "for the crossing."

At this point in the script, the cut and paste Muslim should praise Allah for lending him strength. This man shows no inclination to attribute his strength or survival to mediation divine or otherwise. His protrusive eyes look ready to pop from his skull in fury, as if I've done him some personal harm, though I sense he always speaks bluntly and maybe more so when translating his words.

"You ask me why I left Syria?"

"No," I say, "but—I mean—I would ask."

"I left because my president is trying to kill me. And because ISIL is trying to kill me. And because the Americans"—he blinks, eyelids red, as if unconsciously including me in an accusation he is trying not to spell out—"the Americans are trying to kill me. And the French are trying to kill me. And now the fucking *Russians* are trying to kill me."

Seeing light and feeling heat, I glance to the side: the camera under the rain poncho is nosing in while a crewman gaffs a small arc light above it. The Syrian looks over, clears his throat with the word "enough" and melts back into the crowd. The camera halts, pans away downhill.

At the bottom Jaquon waves a limp, sopping baseball cap and yells up to me, "Let's do it!" The frenzied opening bars of "Brand New Cadillac" rip through the rain as if on cue. I yank back the rope and the refugees start down while I collect their chits, trying to keep count.

Probably the Syrian's brief speech was rehearsed— maybe while bailing out the raft during the crossing this morning? Maybe he sensed that his only chance to deliver it was now—that later, while queued up at European borders, he would be well-advised to say nothing.

While the refugees flow down the five lanes toward the buses, I notice several NGO reps standing around the film crew. There's Andromache—a social worker from Mytilene, the island's capital—who's on subcontract with the UNHCR. Unlike the regular reps with their various team-logoed rain gear, she in her light parka and jeans is sodden, her blond curls pasted flat. She's the only rep not making a point of constantly, flagrantly passing in front of the camera to log media hits for their brand. She smiles gamely and gives me the thumbs-up. I nod back, trying to keep my count.

When I look up again, a Dutch NGO rep across the lane is eyeing me from under the sagging brim of a Tilley hat. "Can we not turn off this *ridiculous* music?" Her pleading eyes are not unkind and for a moment I think I see what they see: OXY's manic, make-do informality, the rutted bus lanes bannered with rags, the shingle overhead with its smiley circle like a sun in a toddler's finger painting, the soggy chits, the shriekingly unsuitable playlist, the volunteers in their unmatching civvies...

Moments later, just after Joe Strummer bawls *Jesus Christ, where d'you get that Cadillac*, her wish is mysteriously granted. The music stops, its raving replaced by scores of voices, English and Arabic overlapping, some arguing ("Stop now, man, I think we're over sixty!" Me: "No, I counted fifty-five!" Jaquon: "Better count again!"), and the rumble of buses, and the lashing patter of rain on mud. I start recounting and discover a note pencilled on a scrap of newsprint: WE THANK YOU. Runnels of muddy water are gushing down the lanes. Somewhere Shayn calls repeatedly, "Mind your step, mates!" And now—just as randomly as it cut out—the music revives, this time a Bollywood dance medley.

Despite the rain and cold, my own discomfort, my concern about the refugees (how can they not be exhausted and hypothermic by now?) and my novice fear of fucking things up, the day has become exhilarating, in fact beautiful. The refugees are clearly pleased, relieved to be making progress. Their feelings are contagious. The young ones high-five me as they stride past. The older men put a hand to their hearts—a gesture I've always loved and now mimic—or else shake my hand and chant, *"Assalamu alaikum!"* A few young men bearing chits for later buses try to push into the queue, but mostly everything clicks along. I'm swaying a little to the Bollywood bass line, in part to keep warm but also because of the unspoken esprit de corps now encompassing both volunteers and refugees.

Night falls early, the rain tapers to a trickle. By 7 p.m. the last available bus groans away and by the time my shift ends, at eleven, just a dozen refugees—three families—remain in OXY. They have one of the space-heated big tops to themselves. Maybe the extra room is a slight consolation; what they wanted, of course, was to move on with the others. We've served hot soup, pita bread and fruit to these few overnight guests, whom we get to pamper.

A car arrives from town and Omiros climbs out of the passenger seat with an unlit cigarette between his lips. He's here for the overnight shift. I and a few others will return to town in the car. I put out my hand for a shake and he counter-offers a fist. As we bump fists, he says in his villainous Spanish basso, "I hear that some refugees will stay here tonight and take a rest."

"They were disappointed at first," I say. "They seem happier now."

"I will go see them. I wish I could speak Arabic." (I keep forgetting that he can't, although his father was Syrian.) "I wish all of them could stay overnight, for a rest. More and more, they go straight to Moria, which is much too full."

He issues me a statutory cigarette (all the volunteers smoke) and while I peer at my fingers holding it, he draws a lighter from his trenchcoat.

"Here, Stavros."

"OK," I inhale. "Thanks."

He lights his own. After a deep drag he says thoughtfully, "In the Arab countries, if I light your cigarette and you are a man, it is a sign of respect. In Spain, if I light your cigarette, it means you are my bitch."

I release the smoke slowly.

"I see it in the Arab way," he says, again proffering his fist.

"Respect," I say and bump the fist.

Tracy Chapman pipes in softly. Frowning, he says, "The NGOs and the Greek authority want the refugees in the official camp as fast as possible. This is sad to me. We have worked so hard to make a warm and cozy place." He pronounces it *cosee* and again I'm struck by the gap between his gangster affect, which he could use to intimidate and dominate, and his tender, maternal impulse to create a nest-like way-station for the homeless.

Adrift in the Dictionary of Origins

I'M WALKING ON THE PIER PAST THE FISHERMEN'S chapel, en route to the Captain's Kitchen to check the schedule. The pier is deserted but for the small wisp of a woman shuffling toward me, looking down at her socked, sandalled feet. Alice. I greet her softly, trying not to alarm her. She looks up: vacant eyes magnified by the large round lenses of her glasses. After a moment she says simply, "Ah."

She too is an earnest amateur of languages. She was a history professor at the University of Bristol and took early retirement some years ago. She now wishes she had studied and taught linguistics. We've spoken a couple of times about our struggles with Greek grammar (fifty-five or so inflections of every verb, instead of four or five as in English).

Attempting to make eye contact, I ask her how it's going at Anastasia House, the clothing depot for the Captain's

Kitchen. Cardboard boxes of donated clothing arrive there daily from all over the world. Alice is said to unpack and sort the stuff with the painstaking care of an Egyptologist uncrating artifacts.

My question appears to stump her. She always looks stumped or troubled, her eyes darting behind those lenses, seeking purchase, settling nowhere—certainly not on the eyes of the person in front of her. Yet you always know she is listening carefully, then responding thoughtfully, if not always to your question.

"I do wonder," she finally blurts. "I mean, it occurs to me. Now that I see you here. We linguists, when we travel—do we simply use a love of words, foreign words, as a way *not* to engage with the country? Engage directly, I mean... yes?"

"You mean—"

"The phrase book—the dictionary! Little walls between us and the living—us and the people around us."

She is speaking and it's thirty years ago, a smoky, low-ceilinged pub half a world from here, where my friend Mark Sinnett—who has an English accent of his own, though of a less patrician grade—is reading me a poem he has drafted. A line leaps clear, encysting itself in a corner of my mind, to emerge at odd times over the years since: *I have hidden too long in the Dictionary of Origins.*

Of course the line leapt clear. It's not only good but also spoke to me of myself. (Maybe every close reader or listener is a narcissist; maybe the poem contained better lines that I missed because they weren't personally diagnostic.) I want to tell Alice I know what she means and recite that line to her. But when I nod and say, "I think that's true, of me at least," she meets my gaze for just a moment and says with terrifying sincerity, "Oh, but you seem to find it so *easy* to connect to others! Enviably so! I see you talking and laughing with them constantly!"

"That's just careful image management," I mutter. Her flummoxed eyes twitch away, toward the empty harbour, and I regret my glib little dodge. Alice operates on a vulnerably earnest level, that of the unselfconscious keener, what I am myself at heart. The persona she has observed—the sanguine sociability, facetious self-mockery, steady eye contact—has taken years to cultivate and will never feel fully natural. How I respect the authenticity of the unprotected nerd, a being I lacked the courage to remain.

Club Compassion vs. Planet Sleep

WET, CHILLED AND HUNGRY AFTER ANOTHER DAY OF rain at the camp, I climb an outside stairway to a restaurant above the town's main street. The place's name, the Hellenic Isles, howls Tourist Trade, hence a less authentic and costlier meal. But it's late, places have closed early, and I'm too cold and tired to look further.

The photographer sits at a corner table in an empty, drafty room, a sleek sliver of a laptop open in front of him. His glowing face, that of a crafty, quarrelsome boy, though one with a stubbly beard, is lowered to the screen. I've never seen him in any other posture. He sits this way for hours at the Captain's Kitchen—alone, corner table—editing his photographs. He's German but goes by the professional name Jack Marvin. Since early October he has been on the island capturing images of the crisis.

Many of his photos, all black and white, are techni-
cally superb and also emotionally forceful, their angles,
framing and chiaroscuro romantic. Yet he himself reads
as bitter skeptic. I have yet to see him smile. The world
beyond his screen, on the rare occasions he looks up (lips
sourly pursed in his black beard, skin a faded grey-white:
the artist as emanation of his own monochrome work),
disappoints and offends him. Or is he suffering from a
version of the hypercriticality that grips writers in the
final throes of an edit? When the search for flaws, line
after line, bleeds over into your life and you find yourself
obsessively cavilling, as if you could correct or redact
the world.

Jack Marvin does not look up from his screen now.
I start toward another table. In the rumbling tone of a
threat he invites me over: "Sit here if you would like." I
pull out the chair across from him. He fixes me with
eyes like small black apertures. I mention the weather—
the rain riveting down into the street beyond the clear
plastic sheeting that is the restaurant's winter walls and
window—and he stares harder.

"Care for wine?" I ask, shivering. "I'm going to get
a half-litre."

"I do not drink. Let me speak frankly. There is a grave
problem with alcohol among the volunteers. For the last
week, people have been arriving late for shifts in the
morning. Perhaps some have even been drunk."

A half smile primps his lips.

"Lindsay tells me the veteran volunteers got really
burned out last month," I say. "When the refugees were
landing by the thousands. So maybe—"

"I know of the thousands. I was here. I was capturing the pictures."

"Maybe now that it's a bit less intense they're collapsing. I mean, because they can. An adrenal collapse—a bit like students after exams."

"I did not say they are 'collapsing.' I said they are getting drunk and sleeping late. On Friday night, many were at the nightclub along this street."

"So I heard."

"You are comparing this stress to examinations for a student?"

"You're right—bad analogy."

He studies my mouth as if waiting for more. Down in the gulley of the street, a car howls past, tires sizzling on the wet pavement.

"When you think about it," I say, "most analogies stink. Still…"

"Your analogy is truly bad."

"… if you can't send volunteers away on leave, like during a war, then burnout is going to happen."

"Now you compare this situation to a war!"

"It's a better analogy. Just look at your photographs. Especially the beach ones. Some look like battle scenes— like stills out of a war film. And people are dying here all the time."

A young waitress appears and stands skittishly clear of the table, terrified of Jack Marvin. He fixes her from under his eyebrows like a headmaster in bifocals. I order wine and spaghetti with clam sauce. Jack Marvin nods at his coffee mug. The waitress retreats.

"May I see the image you're working on?"

He grips the side of the screen, lowers it with a soft click and folds his hands on top. "No."

"Fair enough."

"It will be extremely good," he says. "Also, extremely sad. The ones with the tiny little children... naturally these will be the most... ah..."

"Moving?"

"*Affecting.*"

"Do you have any children of your own?"

He looks at me as if he has never been asked a more preposterous question. The waitress brings the wine, more Nescafé and a basket of bread and butter (not olive oil: sure sign of a tourist joint). She turns and flees.

I nod at the basket: "Help yourself to bread."

"I will be eating no bread."

Still chilled, I slather a slice with a thick impasto of hard butter, yearning for the fat's caloric kick. From outside, tires skidding, horns blatting, then voices shooting it out in Greek and English. I leap up and walk over to the plastic wall. Below in the narrow street, two vehicles are staring each other down, nose to nose, the drivers leaning out their windows and yelling. On the right, a wide delivery truck with PLANET SLEEP inscribed on the side panel. The small driver, his comb-over undone by the rain, pumps his fist and screams, "*Fyge ap'edho, malaka*!" *Get out of here, you wanker!* On the left, blocking him, a blue van with the words CLUB COMPASSION blazoned in white; it must have tried to park in front of the restaurant. Other cars, trapped behind the truck, start sounding their horns. The rain drenches down. The Club Compassion driver slams his horn and shouts back in heavily accented English: "Back off, man! Fuck you anyway!"

Jack Marvin appears beside me, holding his camera, shaking his head. "Not worth a picture, these idiots. This 'Club Compassion'! They are like a Marseilles gang. Always drunk and driving twice the permitted speed. I hear they use cocaine."

"They're a medical outfit?"

"They are adrenalin addicts! They want to arrive first at any rescue! Some say they carry firearms. I doubt this. I agree they work hard."

The Greek truck driver climbs down out of the cab, rakes a hand through his hair and walks toward the van. Its doors fly open and the driver and passenger spring out and rooster toward him. The Greek is smaller, older and outnumbered but uncowed. The young guys wear blue track suits with the hoods up. The trio converge and resume yelling. Another blue-painted vehicle, a Mini Cooper, lurches up and squeals to a stop beside the van, honking in support. The street is blocked in either direction as cars jam up behind the Club Compassion convoy.

"I am going back to my work," Jack Marvin mutters. "Human beings embarrass me."

The pair in blue track suits are returning to their van. The Mini Cooper jerks into reverse; the vehicles clogged behind it have to back up too. The men get into the van, retreat a few car lengths, stop. The truck driver, climbing back up into the cab, bellows, "*Ligo piso, malakes!*" *A little farther, fuckheads!* The van driver leans out, screaming, bucking his own pointing hand like a firing pistol. The Greek sounds his horn, Club Compassion sirens back, both go on honking steadily.

Syria defeats Canada on penalty kicks

UNABLE TO HITCH A RIDE TO THE CAMP—IT'S 7 A.M., no cars yet on the road—I flag down and climb aboard the public bus to Allonia and ask the driver how much he'll charge to drop me at OXY. "*Ela*," he growls, fanning his hand to beckon me, "*katse'dho!*" *Get on, sit here!* I fold down the child-sized shotgun seat as we rumble off. Plastic ikons the size of playing cards sway from the tattered sun visors, the saints' faces morose yet calm, as if resigned to the perils of Greek highways. I smell bittersweet incense; the pair of widows whispering behind me must have attended early mass.

A flimsy guardrail, the cliffs below it, the Aegean beyond. The sea is vacant except for a shark-grey naval ship patrolling the Turkish coastline ten kilometres north. Twenty-four hours ago the Turks accepted an offer from the EU: two billion euros to blockade their own coastline, for now, thus detaining the refugees on that side. Yesterday only three rafts got across the straits, all after dark, the lowest number of the year so far.

The silent driver gives a fellowly nod-and-wink as he drops me off. As I cross the highway—cheered by his gesture and the vision or version of me it conjures: a fine and likeable fellow, a hearty volunteer bounding off his hitched ride and striding into the sleeping camp—there's a flash of movement in the bus's last window. A blurred face, a raised hand. I tip my hat brim, grin and wave. The figure comes into focus. In the receding window's ikon frame, he is not waving but giving me the finger.

The night shift are still asleep on their cots in one of the otherwise-vacant tent shelters. I stand staring in. The earth lurches violently and I'm airborne, swooping, hitting the ground with a chuff of breath. I lie prone, winded, my left cheek and my lips squashed into the gravel. My right arm is torqued behind me. A solid weight pins me in place.

I hear myself say faintly, "Pericles?"

"You see, Stavro, how difficult it would be for any stranger to invade the camp and cause harm?"

"You keep proving it," I say. "May I get up now?"

"Pardon...? Ah, of course!"

As he climbs off my back I add, "I hope Ratko's all right. The big Serbian guy? I hear you sprained his ankle."

"Nonsense! He is fine. I know how to tackle without harm. Unless I need to cause harm. As you know, there are people who would hurt our visitors."

I stand up. Although I'm winded, I am in fact unharmed. My fall was controlled, guided, as if I was being dipped by a ballroom-dancing champion. Pericles pumps my hand and grins up at me, his inflated arms and sandbag thighs packed into a wrestling team track suit oddly accessorized with a trilby hat. He has all but grown a beard overnight. His English is densely accented but good. He was delighted to be hired as OXY's night watchman; his former job, bouncer at the main hotel, was lost with the crisis and the vanishing of the tourists, phenomena he refers to with no detectable air of grievance.

"All quiet here last night?" I ask, picking up my hat and brushing it off.

"Too quiet! I had to walk all night to stay alert. You too must be more alert, Stavro. Ah, may I demonstrate"— pronouncing the first two syllables like *demon*—"a new chokehold I'm trying to learn?"

"I think I'd like to stretch a bit first. Maybe get a coffee."

"Very well then, tomorrow! For now I will go home and sleep."

I climb the portable steps of a dirty, abandoned-looking truck trailer and knock on the door. Two voices yell from inside. I let myself in. The mobile kitchen's interior—unlike its facade—is new, all gleaming sinks, shelves, counters and fridges. A shiny cauldron of lentil stew simmers on a galley stove while latkes brown on a grill. Roddy, the chef, turns from the cauldron and offers me a drink from his mug. Coffee spiked with, I think, gin. He makes further friendly noises. The words are incomprehensible, the accent a mystery. Irish? Welsh? Glaswegian? I'm not even sure he's speaking English. Overnight he will have prepared the usual six hundred servings of the vegetarian stew that the camp has on hand daily. A wiry, concave man in a spattered chef's tunic, his left hand bandaged, he's walleyed and wobbling.

At the grill in a T-shirt and jeans, Danny—strapping, tattooed, mostly toothless—flips the latkes, presumably a snack for him and Roddy. A home-rolled cigarette droops from his underlip. He picks up his mug and nods to me, red-eyed. "Drink up, lad—long day coming." According to Lindsay he has logged some fifty night shifts in a row, mainly at OXY. She keeps begging him to take a night off. Down the length of his triceps I read, WITHOUT OUR BRAIN & MUSCLE NOT A SINGLE WHEEL CAN TURN, with the anarchist *A* as full stop.

I nod toward the cauldron. "You think that many will come today?"

"If not today, soon enough," he says in a Geordie accent. "The Turks have banked their cheque, haven't they? They'll self-blockade for a couple days, then ask the EU for a raise. Here, eat one of these with your victory pills"—a euphemism for lentils among volunteers of the Spanish Civil War—"they're masterful."

And they are.

In the canteen hut I make instant coffee. To Kanella, who has followed me inside, I toss a few slices of processed cheese extracted from a stale sandwich. She traces her ritual three circles before curling up at my feet next to the portable radiator. From my satchel I take the proofs of a novel I'm supposed to be reviewing, its backdrop the Roma holocaust during and after World War II.

At 9 a.m. a bus arrives and we get to work. This group of Syrians crossed by fishing boat, not inflatable raft—perhaps a ruse by the smugglers to fool the Turkish navy. For a while I'm making cheese sandwiches in the canteen, then helping Larry at the wicket distribute the sandwiches along with bananas and bottled water. Once everyone has had at least something to eat and drink, we'll commence the slower process of dishing up bowls of the lentil stew.

This group seems almost cheerful. Having crossed on a proper boat must be a factor, though there's also the bright sun after days of rain, and the relative emptiness, hence spaciousness, of the camp. The queue is amiably patient, as if people realize there is no hurry, there will be food and space for everyone. Larry and I find our rhythm and now I hear him—behind me, slapping together more sandwiches while I pass them out through the wicket—softly whistling "King of the Road."

This work, which I love, is the pure antithesis of my work at home. The writing life is solitary; this is dynamically social. The writing life is staggered with doubt and procrastination; here, when a crowd queues up, or, more urgently, a raft comes ashore, dithering is impossible.

The rush is over and Larry, in his beret, whistling as he tidies the canteen, shoos me away like a testy but good-hearted uncle. "Here—keys to the camper. Go give Chet Baker a couple slices of this awful cheese. Then find the soccer ball, behind the passenger seat, and see if any of these kids want to play."

"You going to join us?"

"Wouldn't hear of it, Steve. My sporting days are over. Get out of here."

Ten minutes later I approach one of the large tents. Many of the Syrians are just inside, sitting on chairs or on the woven sleeping mats, some eating, some lying down. Others are sitting out on the benches against the tent's white plastic walls, tilting their faces, eyes closed, toward the low but warm sun.

In the mouth of the big top I hold up the ball and call out, "Anyone want to play?" Instantly three children leap up and start toward me—a boy of around twelve years old, another around ten, and a girl of six or seven. We set up in front of the field kitchen trailer. I drag a steel crowd-control fence into place for a net. The boys mime that they consider it rather small but it will do.

At first, the game pits the two smaller children versus the elder. I play goalkeeper for both sides. I'm no soccer player and have little idea what I'm doing. They do. Even the smallest, the girl, can kick with some force if little accuracy. But it's the middle child—blue T-shirt, jeans, dirty trainers too big for him—who can really dribble and drill his shots with precision. His grin is spirited, almost taunting. The three race around in front of me, the girl falling a couple of times, crying momentarily, getting up and rejoining the game. Behind them the parents have emerged from the tent to join the other Syrians on the benches, where they all sprawl in the sun, watching the action with faint, fatigued smiles.

It hits me that the children, too, have just crossed the border straits on a dinghy steered by a refugee who might never have seen the sea before. The kids' resiliency may have more to do with ignorance than youth; they have no idea what they've just survived; they must feel their parents would not lead them into dangers over which they, the parents, had no control. As for the steersman randomly appointed by the traffickers, in the children's eyes he too must have seemed a competent adult. Or have such illusions already been shattered, at least in the oldest one's mind? He has a face crowded with hard cares, lessons gleaned too early in the cram-school of a war zone.

The kids hold a penalty kick shootout, heel-clearing a spot in the gravel, fussily placing the ball, quibbling over the placements and whether a shot that smacks the edge of the fence should count. I don't understand the words but can follow the negotiations. The kickers whoop and cheer when they score. A few adults clap or chuckle. Larry, smoking a pipe, watches and calls, "Careful now, kids!" when they slip on the gravel, and, to me, "Careful of your back, Steve!" Omiros, the Lion of OXY, looms along in his flapping trenchcoat and aviator shades, steps into the fray, steals the ball and chips it past my hand. He nods to me and bids the awestruck children *salam*, then swaggers on toward the lower parking lot, where an empty bus should soon be appearing.

By 1 p.m. the Syrians are boarding and a handful of volunteers stand in the dirt of the parking lot to see them off. The ten-year-old boy in his blue T-shirt, sitting on his mother's lap, has pressed his face to the window and keeps grinning and waving at me. He's holding one of the red, heart-shaped balloons that we handed out to the children as they boarded; someone in Poland mailed a box of them to the Captain's Kitchen. I lose sight of the mother and son, then there they are in the open doorway of the bus. The boy waves again, I wave back, then he leaps down and sprints toward me, the balloon on its string jigging behind him like a kite. He stops in front of me, lifts his small hand for another formal shake and then, with his left, proffers the balloon and nods firmly. Again imitating the Muslims who've thanked me for one thing or another, I put my left hand over my heart (should it be my right?) and accept the gift. "*Shukhran*," I say. He turns and runs back to the juddering bus, his mother in the doorway beckoning as she happily scolds him. *Come, my love, hurry!*

So a day that began with a snapshot of seething local animus ends as a kind of idyll, the setting sun warm, the camp serenely still after being vigorously, usefully occupied. The bus disappears around a mountainside to the south and I assume the soccer players are on their way to wherever in northern Europe their parents hope to claim asylum.

Now—April 2020—I wonder if they even made it out of Greece and into Macedonia before that border and others to the north crashed closed. With luck, the three are now kicking a ball around on a windswept pitch beside a very different body of water, the North Sea or the Baltic. But they might well be interned in one of the growing refugee "hot spots" of Greece, still awaiting a decision on their asylum claim or, if rejected, living there as prisoners while lacking access to such amenities of modern prisons as showers, flush toilets, libraries, clean water.

I stay after my shift to talk to Lindsay, Omiros, Asim, Pilar and Larry, and we share an early supper, Kanella ecstatically helping us to make inroads on the surfeit of lentil stew. The crags behind the camp glow with the setting light and echo Pink Floyd's *Dark Side of the Moon* while a cold wind, after two days' calm, blows south across the straits.

2. INTERMISSION

DECEMBER 6, 2015, BRUSSELS: *Today the EU announced that it is close to agreeing a more formal, long-term arrangement with Turkey to prevent Syrian and other asylum seekers from entering Europe through Greece. The deal will provide money and resources to help Turkey host the migrants in camps there. Nikos Theofilakis, a Greek economist critical of the initial 2-billion-euro deal, complained that the EU is providing little help to Greece. "Tens of thousands of refugees are here," he said, "and many more will come. The austerity measures [of the EU, the IMF, and the World Bank] have already reduced Greece to a condition of debt serfdom. This deal, which does not include Greece, can only make the situation worse for all."*

* * *

Human rights don't stop at borders; neither do international laws. When someone is desperate enough to attempt to cross the world's deadliest migration routes, it usually means something is very wrong. Imagine a fear big enough to drive you to leave everything you know to get into some crook's rickety boat to cross the Mediterranean—to risk not only your life but the lives of your children. Imagine preparing for a journey by taking contraceptives in the knowledge that you might well be raped.

—*Dr. Tom de Kok, MSF (Médecins Sans Frontières)*

Lifelines

ANOTHER DENSE CLUSTER OF PASSENGERS IS GLIDING
beachward but this time their flimsy vessel is not just low
in the water but beneath it. Sixty disembodied heads-and-
torsos, men, women, children, approach as if they are seated
on the top deck of a U-boat. Instead of calling out excit-
edly, encouragingly, we volunteers simply stare. The raft's
pneumatic compartments are so deflated, or the craft so
overladen, that its bow and sides are submerged. The motor
too must be largely immersed but is still throbbing away.

I don't think I saw this. I saw overpacked dinghies
come ashore with just inches of freeboard—as on the beach
at Skala on my fourth night—and I heard reports of others arriving more or less submerged, and I pictured that,
described it to others, dreamed it. Did I actually see it? I
doubt we volunteers would have been so quiet as the raft

approached. We never were. But above all, it's the silence of the immersed refugees that makes me doubt the scene. Where is the vocal crescendo as they reach toward safety with excited, relieved greetings or panicked screams? Sometimes volunteers screamed or shouted too. As if no one on either side could bear simply to watch the closing gap close—to trust the inevitable momentum of the process. All had to cast their voices seaward or shoreward like lifelines.

I wake at wolflight, 7 a.m. Bitter residue of a prescription hypnotic coating my tongue; irrelevant sleep-erection of a single man in a rented room.

I dress quickly in the cold, stumble outside and draw the sun into my eyes like breath into lungs after a dive. The white balcony is already warm. I bring out a heel of bread, olive oil, a pomegranate, Greek coffee and the notebook in which I mean to bullet-point the last few days. Downstairs, Elektra keeps emerging to sweep her doorstep and forecourt with mounting vehemence. She wants me to clear off so she can inspect my room, strip the bed of its extra blankets and fold and fiercely re-shelve them in the wardrobe.

The woman in the room next to mine comes out, lights a cigarette and pulls up a chair. At seventy-one, Clara Romero is the oldest of the volunteers. She has the lean, leathered aspect of a lifelong venturer in countries that tourists seldom brave. Blue jeans, plain white T-shirt, sunglasses. Thick hair, still striated with black, tied back in a pigtail. She has been teaching English to adult students in Albania but came here, she says, because it wasn't far to come, her school gave her a leave of absence, and it seemed the least she could do.

I cleave the pomegranate and pass half across the table along with a small spoon.

"I wish I had the patience," she says in a tobacco-cured rasp. "As fruits go, they're an aesthetic triumph but a functional failure."

"I'm hoping they'll teach me to take my time—to be more mindful."

"Oh, mindfulness is so overrated! Just live your life. Who *cares* if you're impatient or get distracted?"

Over a second cigarette she reveals that her lover in Albania is a mountain bandit currently doing time in a maximum-security institution outside Tirana. Her adult daughter is a graduate student in the States, where Clara comes from originally and somewhat apologetically. She refers now to Donald Trump and his unlikely, in fact Vonnegutian, presence in a presidential race. I tell her Larry believes Trump hasn't a chance in hell. Clara remains worried. She embodies a paradox typical of the older volunteers, who combine the energy and resolve of optimists with the anxiety of pessimists.

We act as if we can make a difference; we worry it's all in vain.

The sun is scorching, the air icy, as on a high desert plateau. A winter chill lurks in the shadows under the table where I'm kneading my quads, still aching from the soccer.

"Smoke?" she says, offering her pack.

I tell her I'm rolling my own, a couple a day, now that I realize tobacco is a key feature of the Mediterranean diet.

"You haven't been talking to that lunatic Darren, have you? He's been rolling them since he decided Big Tobacco is partnering with the Viagra folks, putting saltpetre in the cigarettes." Conspiracy theories run rampant among the volunteers: contrails as the vapour of brainwashing sprays, moon landings faked in floodlit hangars in the Utah desert, the Great Zionist Banking Confederacy.

She and I will be working the afternoon shift, starting at 3 p.m., though in different places—she at OXY, I at Anastasia House, the stately old limestone building where Alice the linguist has been sorting donated clothing. When I admit I'm not looking forward to my first shift there, since curating or clotheslining pants, socks and sweaters is not something I could ever find interesting, she says she feels the same. "But last week, what do you know, I warmed up to it. Time passes so slowly there—and that turns out to be a nice break. Don't get me wrong, mostly I *like* time, I like moving through it—I don't mind that it moves quick and sweeps me along—that's *exciting*. But that place... it's a refuge."

Ornate, archaic wooden doors open onto a grand atrium that ends in a tall south-facing window. The atrium is flooded with winter sunlight. Large, lofty rooms open to either side. This building, long disused, might once have been a rich family's mansion or an imposing administrative structure of some kind.

It seems Alice has had to return to the UK, her departure another instance of the high rate of turnover among volunteers. The new supervisor is a Greek who has lived on the island for all her fifty years. Hard times, she says, have come and gone before, but never has she seen such a time as this. Before replacing Alice, Natasha held one of the few paid jobs at OXY, cleaning and maintaining the toilets. Probably the Captain's Kitchen foundation assumed that middle-class foreigners, however robust their idealism, would balk at the job. Some days in early fall, several thousand refugees, many of them ill, visited the plywood washroom shed on their way through OXY... Still, I think the foundation was wrong. Many of us would have been willing, if unenthusiastic. For her part, Natasha says she was grateful for the work: "Yes, of course it was hard in many ways, but they were good people. We laughed and we cried."

Within an hour of meeting her, I think of her as the Simone Weil of Lesvos—emaciated, self-effacing, quite possibly saintly. In both her movements and her speech she is quiet and deliberate, as if concentrating equally hard on every step, every word. Because her English is strong I don't need to strain her patience with my dubious Greek— though if anyone would have the patience, she would.

She asks if I would open some of the cardboard boxes full of warm clothing sent from around the world—Iceland, Norway, Germany, Canada, even Louisiana (where in Baton Rouge did they find all these winter woollens?). In the grand, drafty atrium, on a carpenter's table, I slit open boxes with a paring knife. The wall is plastered with donation cover letters, many of them illuminated with children's drawings: crayon rainbows over tall, teetery houses, toothy suns, a stick-figure family wearing toques and mittens. The notes are mostly in English: *We hope this scarfs will help some children be warm on their long walk!* A few are in German and one in a language I've never seen before. Lithuanian?

In a bubble-lined manila envelope postmarked Rotterdam, three small pairs of hand-knitted mittens: white snowmen on an evergreen background.

I sit on the floor of a high-ceilinged storeroom and begin sorting. All these things will be urgently needed; the sunlight sloping in now is brilliant but the air outside is cool and these unheated stone rooms are cold. And this is Greece, and barely December. The refugees are headed north into winter of a starker kind. Chilled where I sit, I pull over my own layers an ugly but thick carotene-coloured sweater, one that a refugee will soon be wearing.

The morning passes at a geological pace. I am to weed out any hats, scarves or sweaters not substantial enough for winter conditions. Though deeply bored, I try to concentrate; negligent triage could mean serious trouble for travellers in January on the many-bordered journey north.

I use a tall wooden ladder to retrieve plastic storage bins from the top shelf, almost twenty feet up, bring them down, repack and in some cases reclassify them with sticky labels and a gel pen, then replace them on the shelves. Since Alice's departure, it seems, the shelving system has grown not only less formal but less confident (WARM HATS THE LITTLE BABY?, reads one label, and another, SWETTERS MAYBE THE BIGGER DAMES).

Slumped and mouth-breathing, I check my watch again. Clara has described this place as a retreat from our era's hurtling hyperkinesis. As my lethargy deepens I wonder if I'm now beyond such retreats, addicted to the body's own uppers, fully a creature of our time. *Is* the quest for adrenalin the true reason some have come here as seemed the case with Club Compassion? As for me, twenty-five years of triaging words and ideas, rarely seeing the effort's human effect, have roused a hunger for embodiment, belonging, rooted usefulness.

At noon a car pulls up on the steep cobbled street beyond the open front doors. Natasha and I unload a dozen heavy garbage bags stuffed with wet, discarded clothing sent from OXY, where a hundred Syrians have been bused after being rescued from a sinking raft off Efthalou Beach.

On clotheslines in the stone-walled yard, she and I hang out all the soaked, soiled clothing we can salvage. Though I'm awake now and glad to be working more actively out in the warmer air, this task is challenging in its own way: several times in the first minutes I have to manage my distaste as I handle some piece of clothing that smells strongly of urine or, more faintly, shit. (The latter we throw out instead of sending on to the laundry.) I'm tempted to go back into the house for rubber gloves but Natasha, hanging things steadily and impassively, is not bothering. To flee and leave her working while I go in search of gloves will feel fussy as well as lazy. (Just wash your hands after you finish.) Once more I'm trying to rally a mental and moral discipline, to fully assign myself to an unglamorous task.

For some weeks now, despite Natasha's efforts, a neighbour's dog has been slipping into the yard and stealing some of the shoes set out to dry. Hiram is a portly, short-legged terrier with an outsized head and anthropoid eyes, the irises brown, the whites flashing expressively whenever he looks at us sidewise, checking, awaiting his chance. "Somewhere," Natasha says, "there is a secret nest of shoes." (How I envy this choice of word: nest.) Hiram only ever poaches one shoe from any pair, and so has rendered some two dozen pairs useless. Natasha seems to find this loss perfectly natural, part of the attrition one expects in an imperfect world of conflicting desires. "Go away now, *fyge!*" she scolds him. She can barely contain her smile. "Such an awful dog you are!" Hiram waddles backward through the gate and lies down, head between his paws, watching us, biding his time.

At Anastasia House only two or three workers are on at once, so the shifts are few. I don't realize it as I leave at 3 p.m., but my first day here is also to be my last. Life spends decades terracing complexity into the people you meet only in passing; on Lesvos, in the flux of the crisis, this truth seems truer by the day. Natasha will be another of the long-term volunteers—heroes, in my mind—I will see just once or twice and not again.

Efthalou Beach

NO RAFTS HAVE SLIPPED THROUGH THE TURKISH blockade for over twenty-four hours, and tonight the Efthalou Beach crew is skeletal. I and a young Welshman named Harry Evans are sitting outside under a bare trellis beside an olive grove and the atelier of the expatriate artist Nigel Housman. We're on call, a five-minute walk uphill from the beach, where one other volunteer, Jaquon, is tending a beacon fire of discarded life vests.

Housman and his wife Vera and daughter Athena, who have lived here for many years, have involved themselves in the crisis from the outset. Over the last year they have helped refugees on the beach and sheltered them up here in their bungalow and the atelier; they have hosted Captain's Kitchen volunteers on day and night shifts, urging them to help themselves to tea and biscuits and to sit under the trellis or nap in the olive grove; and along with the volunteers they've constructed a framewood-and-tarpaulin depot for spare clothing.

Housman is an edgy, vexed, outspoken man with Rod Stewart hair and a *Coronation Street* accent. In the atelier where volunteers are free to make tea with the electric kettle and use the toilet or shower, he carves olive wood into anything from key fobs to large, elaborate sculptures based on Greek myths. The finished wood bears a resemblance to mahogany but has a distinctive, pleasantly bitter scent.

For him, as for any extrovert raconteur, other people's words serve as mere punctuation, cues or click-on-links for his monologues. Fresh auditors like me are an occasion for rehashing stories and reprising grievances. In his case, these mostly feature him and his family as isolated heroes thwarted in their efforts to help refugees by a corrupt local bureaucracy, an idle constabulary, and venal, xenophobic villagers. Harry, familiar with the routine, keeps quietly excusing himself and ducking into the atelier to boil more water for the pot. Meanwhile Housman looms over me, gripping the edge of the trellis above him as if about to perform pull-ups, his patter accelerating, gaining volume.

But there are worse things to be than a generous, hospitable blowhard; and maybe these tales of embattled valour reflect a veteran's natural impulse to remind recruits of their status—to reinforce a hierarchy of experience necessary in urgent situations. Or is he suffering a kind of post-traumatic mania? He says he has pulled more than one body up onto the sand. And last winter, he adds, tears brightening his eyes, his daughter swam out to a sinking raft and saved the life of a child.

He is proud of her as a musician, too. His stories done
for now, he snaps her newly cut CD into a heritage boom
box, turns it up loud and bangs back into his workshop.
The moment the short record ends, he strides back out and
puts it back on.

Harry is the veteran volunteer at Efthalou. Through the
late summer and fall he has, among other things, helped
get tens of thousands of people onto buses for the twelve-
minute ride to OXY. A husky ex-rower and -rugby player,
he was working on a master's in history when he decided,
more or less overnight, to come here. That was just over
three months ago—not a hundred days—yet he seems
utterly depleted. Though the skin of his handsome face is
lineless, his trimmed beard ungreying, under the deep ledge
of his eyebrows the eyes are dull, eclipsed. His slack features
expressionless. Picture a stunned young officer of exactly a
century ago, on leave after a first tour of duty in Flanders.

In fact, Harry will go on leave tomorrow, a few days off,
his first since arriving. So now, as we try to stay warm with
another pot of tea, he wearily, vaguely instructs me on the
bus-loading protocol. I tell him I get it, though I don't, then
I change the subject to rugby, to distract and divert him.

"Who did you play for?" I ask over the catchy, exuberant
pop songs.

"Well… my university. My university team."

"Sure, I figured that. But which school?"

"Well…" He mumbles something.

"Sorry?"

"Oxford."

The wind is from the north, off the sea, and rising. A
thermometer on the atelier's windowsill shows the mercury

dipping toward a freeze. Harry murmurs that we should go down now and spell off Jaquon.

We walk down a lane winding between stone walls. There are olive groves on either side, though in this darkness the trees can only be heard, wind torqueing the branches and coursing through the leaves. So far, Harry's speech has amounted to a few clipped replies, muted observations, and ellipses lapsing into silence. Now suddenly he is talking about the night in October when several rubber boats capsized and scores of drowned or near-drowned Syrians were rushed into Mithymna harbour: "That night there was no moon either. And it was windy like this. Worse. We'd hoped nobody meant to cross, then we got word." (On this downslope my boot heels are snapping; the bigger man's steps are silent as a wraith's.) "We were on the pier, waiting on the pier. We saw the coast guard pull out in a hurry, then a few of the fishing boats. So we knew there was trouble." (A silence punctuated by the sound of my steps, which I'm trying to dampen.) "One of the fishing boats came back first. Those cats, the ones who wait there? They scattered as if they knew. Then the boat pulled in and we saw the bodies."

The fishermen were shouting, arguing as they lifted people over the decks and onto the pier, the volunteers helping. A second fishing boat docked and you could see the lights and hear the engine of the coast guard ship coming in fast. Within minutes the pier was thronged with people running and yelling or standing dumbstruck or kneeling beside sprawled figures or straddling them and pumping their chests. Some of the figures were very small. The only comparable scene Harry can think of: a riot he once witnessed after a football match in Leeds, when the drunker,

more militant fans of each side waged a street battle. All the individual fights ended up on the ground, one man on top of another, punching, the man on the ground either struggling or lying horribly, helplessly still.

We reach the T-junction where the lane meets the road running along the beach. A restaurant on the corner is now the headquarters of a Dutch medical unit, closed for the night. Harry says, "Lindsay was there. You know what she's like. Never stopped once. Belinda and Tassos were trying to help too—the couple who own the restaurant?"

"I've seen them. I haven't met them."

"It all happened right there. Around those tables they set out on the pier."

"You lost a lot of people that night, didn't you?"

"Funny I can still sit out there and have a pint. Not that it feels the same."

I want to know if he was one of the volunteers trying to resuscitate victims, but it doesn't feel right to ask. As if reading into my reticence, he says, "Managed to save one man. Well, he might have made it anyway. Lost someone else, though."

It was a child, I hear it in his voice.

"Did the CPR for twenty minutes. Maybe more. The boy was gone but the father was right there. I couldn't bear to give up." His voice thickens and clots on the last words. We're walking along the road, toward the beacon fire, Harry trying to light a cigarette.

"I'm sorry," I say.

"Haven't had time to think much about it, really. Had a lot of twelve-hour days there for a bit." We're passing under an amber street light and the deep shadows voiding

his eyes make him appear, as he sounds, years older than his age. He tries again to light up, mutters something and flings the plastic lighter into an oil drum full of garbage. "Frankly," he says, "we have more volunteers than we need right now. Didn't have enough then."

"I know. I'm sorry."

"What?" He stops and frowns, perplexed, as if I've posed a question he can't make sense of.

"It's all right," I say.

"This is the post where they'll queue up. You'll collect the chits from them here. I mean, if any arrive in the next days."

"Here," I say, offering my lighter, but he's kneeling down beside the pile of discarded life jackets heaped against the oil drum. The unlit cigarette hangs from his lips. There's a multi-tool in his hand. He deploys the knife and, bafflingly, says, "Just to give an example. See how many it takes." He seizes a life vest, pins it under his knee and rips into it, slashing toward his leg, the blade cutting through to the road, where it grates sickeningly.

"Closed-cell foam," he says softly. "The real thing." He takes a second vest and performs the same violent operation. This time there's a popping, like a firing cap pistol. "That didn't take long," he says. He lifts the thing into the light, his face turning up toward me, the cigarette barely moving as he speaks. "Have a look. Bubble wrap." He's bending the vest to expose and widen the incision: slashed, deflated plastic protruding, glistening like entrails. "Wouldn't float a house cat. Ten euros, these cost in the markets over there. Next one might be stuffed with cardboard. We've seen sawdust too. Sawdust! Jaquon and I were betting last time we

were down here. I came out a few euros up." He drops the gutted vest in the oil drum. On the dark sea, whitecaps are scrolling shoreward like credits down a screen. "Too soft, deep down, Jaquon. Needs to bet more against human nature. That's the ticket."

By means of the sea

EFTHALOU BEACH, THE MORNING WATCH. A DISMAL
lid of cloud slides low overhead, north to south. The shale-
dark sea is churning and fractious; among the whitecaps
an ice floe or two would not look out of place.

I've built a fire using straw clawed out of a bogus life
vest, splinters from the floorboard of a raft, and a (highly
flammable) authentic life vest. Then a split of olive wood
from the Housman atelier. Across the channel, against a
backdrop of snow-powdered mountains, Turkish ships are
prowling up and down the coast. Thousands are said to be
sleeping rough over there, in olive groves or scrubby woods,
waiting for a chance to cross over. I'm wearing a black wool
scarf, wool toque, and several layers under my leather jacket.
A few others are up at the atelier for tea and food.

On this third day of inactivity I'm trying to coax myself out of a deepening ennui of inertia. Part of the job, I tell myself, is simply being here at my post in case something does happen. They also serve who only stand and wait, etcetera.

This morning when I arrived at the atelier, a few volunteers, bustling and bright-eyed, were tearing through the wetsuits racked outside the storehouse, trying to find their size. Delilah, a tall and volubly confident dramaturge from Chicago, announced that they would be leaving on the 9 a.m. ferry with a Norwegian outfit called Drapen i Havet (Drop in the Ocean). Refugees were now arriving on Xios, an island to the south, and the situation was urgent. Gripping the loose pelt of a wetsuit she ducked into a washroom the size of a phone booth and burst out transformed: an action figure, an aquatic superheroine. Her excitement, her impetuous storm-chasing, might have struck me as indecent and flighty, but in fact I felt envious and for some moments considered finding a wetsuit and shipping out for Xios myself.

Hunched on the beach with my back to the wind, I open my notebook, wishing for fingerless gloves. Eastward I can make out the first of the lookout posts between here and Skala: the flickering of fire on a high sea-cliff. Signal fires, lookout towers—the logistical means here are decidedly analogue. In 1922–23, when my distant relations along with a million other Asian Greeks fled across these straits, they too would have steered toward fires on these beaches and cliffs. (So too, perhaps, the fugitive survivors of Troy, millennia away in time but just thirty miles north up the Asian coast.)

I'm thinking of the '22 crossings because as I sit—face braising, back freezing—I'm trying to read and translate a prose passage by the Greek poet Kostas Karyotakis. In the mid-1920s Karyotakis was working, miserably, as a legal clerk in Preveza, a small city in western Greece. One of his duties was registering refugees from Asia Minor, mainly Greek but also Armenian, and seeing that they were housed in "temporary" camps.

A Helpful Death

Her clothes had neither shape nor colour. I have no idea what she was wearing on her head. She came into the office holding two small children and trailing four others. Each cried or clamoured in a distinctive way. Some were tugging at her skirts, others at her hair. A boy, about three years old, was racked by an oddly silent sobbing. All of them—a frightful orchestra—watched their mother as if she were conducting a symphony. She, however, had lost her score, here in this smart little mahogany office.

She stood before us with wide open eyes. With a kind of phony laughter, a grimace of pitying self-contempt, she explained her reasons. She was Armenian. Her husband had died in a village near here and she had come seeking bread for her children. Now she was pleading for shelter. Someone who knew her language told her there was no space in the camp. When she didn't want to understand, they took her outside into the corridor. There she stayed, spread out on the floor with her children until midday. Next day, same story.

She came many times like that.

At last, they tossed her into a large storeroom. The thirty families staying in there had devised separate little household spaces by means of ingenious walls. Wooden chests, packages, bedsheets and blankets strung up, stacked firewood—all these formed squares, like the defensive squares of a desperate last stand. In these refuges, these little nests, the residents remained motionless or, if they moved, cast mournful shadows on the walls. Scattered between soiled clothing and the remnants of old furniture, they murmured what might have been fairy tales for the children, quietly trying to dispel the dark.

Now the storeroom shines with the light of a single candle. A bundle wrapped with clean white cloth has been placed carefully on the floor, at right angles to the wall. It's the youngest of the Armenian's six children, who died a few hours after they settled in. His siblings are outside playing in the sun. His mother—in fact relieved—watches over her baby for the last time. The other women all envy her, if unmaliciously; starting tomorrow, she will be able to take on work. She herself seems almost pleased. And the dead one waits with such dignity.

Karyotakis committed suicide in 1928. First he tried to drown himself in the sea off Preveza, but he was too skilled a swimmer and, despite his best efforts, kept rescuing himself. After ten hours he gave up—a setback so mordantly amusing to him that he went home and added a postscript to his suicide note: *I would advise all those who are good swimmers never to try to kill themselves by means of the sea…* Next he purchased a revolver—in the photographs of his corpse, it looks too dainty to kill anything—but couldn't get it to work, so he returned to the gunsmith to complain and was duly instructed on the mechanism of the safety catch. Finally he returned to the café and the table where, each day after work, he would sit writing and rewriting his poems, and there he shot himself in the heart.

He was never on Lesvos but—sympathetic to the plight of the Asian Greek refugees—he would have known of these waters, this crossing. He would have known, too, that those refugees were not exactly welcomed here. It might seem odd, Greek-speaking Christians receiving a colder welcome on Lesvos than the non-Greek-speaking Muslims of today, but in the wake of the 1922 catastrophe Greece was even more depressed, economically and spiritually, than now. To the Greeks of that time, the strangers crowding their piers were a daily reminder of defeat and humiliation and seemed apt to overwhelm and further impoverish the country.

These Muslim strangers, on the other hand, have no interest in staying. They want to move on into northern Europe, especially Germany. The cynic's view is that the current Greek helpfulness and *philoxenia*—hospitality—is really a way of sticking it to the Germans and the EU. Well, possibly. Sly strategies are as Greek as *philoxenia*; and I have cousins who talk about Greek Alzheimer's, a form of dementia where you forget everything but the grudges.

Nice ride

WITH CYRUS, THE YOUNG FARSI INTERPRETER, I'M walking to OXY along the highway. We'll be starting at three in a camp that's mostly deserted. The day has brought a reprise of last week's mild weather, hence this leisurely hike along the guardrailed cliff with sea views gaping and shimmering. We're in T-shirts and jeans, our jackets thumb-hitched over our shoulders, his porkpie hat tipped back off his brow.

Ten minutes to go until the camp—one more full curve in the highway—when a Toyota Land Cruiser blazoned with the logo of a major NGO pulls up beside us and purrs along at our speed. Through the closed windows, passengers examine us as if we're the exotic, possibly dangerous animal inmates of a safari park. The front window slides down. A man with a receding hairline and trimmed, greying beard, wearing a logoed windbreaker, articulates slowly, "You two men should not be here. You must be in the *camp*. This is not a safe place for you. Have you registered yet? Do you speak English?"

Without missing a beat, Cyrus says in his flawless American English, "Nice ride, mister. You got room? How about a lift?"

The man's eyes widen, his face recoils. Cyrus is toying with him; now and then, NGO staff in their luxury jeeps give rides to volunteers—most of whom look European— but never refugees. The vehicle accelerates slightly. Cyrus and I accelerate. The man says, "We're in a bit of a hurry, I'm afraid. Not much room…"

Cyrus starts jogging beside the car, his grin very white in his soft black beard. "For real, man—it's just the two of us! I've never been in one of these!"

The window slides up as the Land Cruiser quietly, discreetly accelerates—easing away from us as if pretending not to escape at all. To peel away from refugees walking along the highway might seem both discourteous and undignified.

"Hey, come on!" Cyrus calls after them, waving his hat above his head. "What about that ride, motherfuckers?"

Sacrifice in Greek

IPHIGENIA'S FAVOURITE RESTAURANT HERE IS THE Alonia, a sprawling place at the edge of town on the road to Efthalou Beach, beside the sanctuary for retired donkeys. The Alonia could hold a hundred diners or more but these days is always close to empty except for a few tables around the woodstove. Tonight, despite the cold, the front door is propped open. From outside come the dry heaving of the donkeys' brays and the grinding of the oil press in the work shed of the farmers' collective across the road. Harvest time; night and day the conveyor belt is feeding olives, black, green, russet, purple, into the crusher that chugs and rattles and gushes out a constant stream of chartreuse oil. Tonight at the Alonia, every drop of the delectably pungent oil you sop up with your bread was still inside the fruit this morning.

Four of us are sitting by the stove, thawing ourselves and eating after a slow day at OXY. From the restaurant's Bluetooth speaker come wolfman growls and grunts—the Cretan folksinger Psarantonis, as Iphigenia explains. (Whether there are tourists around or not, the music almost everywhere is contemporary or traditional Greek, not US or European pop.)

Iphigenia lives in rural Connecticut but was born and raised here on Lesvos in such rustic circumstances that one of her earliest memories is of goats waking her at dawn by chewing her hair. The family goats (*de goats*, she calls them, as if her mother tongue was French, not Greek) shared the house with them, especially in winter. The goats, in truth, were mainly confined to her room. "All right, all right," she adds—pausing to set up the punchline—"it was derr room too." As we laugh, she protests with stage indignation that the experience was traumatic—she remains terrified of goats and shuns their products, goat milk, feta cheese, angora sweaters... Her gracefully greying hair is waist-long and, yes, she grows it out to reclaim it from those childhood tormentors who would chew, rend, and stain it grass-green.

The owner brings a complimentary round of rakis for dessert. Larry's brush moustache twitches as he sniffs his glass and says, "I figure the Turks'll let their blockade spring a few leaks any day now, then extort another ransom to plug it up."

"Sounds plausible," I say.

Iphigenia nods. "Any of you know what *rousfetia* is?"

"I had to look it up the other day," I say. "It's a bribe arranged according to certain rules here, right? Like a bribery code?"

"Doesn't sound much different than Washington," Larry says.

"Vienna also!" says Klea, a wiry, intense pediatrician I've seen around but haven't worked with yet.

"Actually, it's Turkish," says Iphigenia. "We got it from dem."

"The word, you mean, or the corruption?" Klea asks.

"Both, both! It all comes from Turkey originally."

"But you just denied that this *cuisine* came from them!" Larry says, indicating our emptied bowls of hummus and taramasalata.

"I deny it again now"—Iphigenia claps a hand to her chest—"and with all my heart! These dishes could not be more Greek. The Lebanese, the Egyptians, the Jews—they all try to claim them! Such flagrant lies!"

She's enjoying herself immensely; she rattles off a description of the many courses served at her wedding banquet, then tells us how her father—an Orthodox priest and New Testament scholar now living in Boston—had first greeted her fiancé at the door: by punching him in the mouth. "At that moment," Iphigenia says, "I knew it would work. That punch was a welcome to the family: we accept you! But it was also a warning to treat me well."

(*Philoxenia* and the darker passions are never far apart. In 1960 my mother had to flee her outraged community in Ottawa, and the private detective they had hired, so as to marry my non-Greek father. They eloped to a remote gold-mining town in northern Ontario, where he found an entry-level teaching job. I was born soon afterward. I took after my mother's kin. Polaroids were duly sent south. In next to no time the Greeks, appeased to see their DNA ascendant, revoked their grudges and opened their hearts and their homes.)

The old man at the next table faces the stove but seems to monitor us out of the corner of his leaky eye. He wears the timeless uniform of the Greek coffee house habitué: a fisherman's cap, dark blazer with patched elbows, a pilled sweater, scuffed dress shoes. He's smoking hand-rolled cigarettes and sipping a cloudy ouzo on ice. An amber-stained grey moustache on a sun- and wind-blasted face. White whiskers sprouting from ears and nostrils.

"So how is your Greek coming along?" Iphigenia asks, trying to sound polite and not look pitying. Any time I've tried to explain to a Greek that my mother rarely spoke *Ellinika* at home, so I'm only now learning, I get the same scornfully incredulous looks: how could his mother have failed to teach him the world's most important language? And if he's half-Greek, why can he not learn it now within a couple of weeks? He must be a fool.

"*Siga siga,*" I say: little by little.

"You have to get your head into the game, Stavro!"

"But I think maybe I figured something out today. The word for sacrifice is *thysia*, right?"

"*Bravo!*"

"So, I'm wondering if it could be related to Theseus— from the myth?"

The old man is definitely auditing the conversation. He squints as he takes a drag on his cigarette and then, as he exhales, half smiles.

"I mean, he's sent to Crete by his father—the king—as a kind of sacrifice to the Minotaur, right?"

"You know your myths better than your Greek," Iphigenia says.

"So, maybe the name is constructed out of the word for sacrifice?"

Iphigenia shrugs. "My father is interested in that stuff."

The man is slowly shaking his head, looking straight at me, displaying long, discoloured teeth. The wide gap between the incisors lends his grin a note of mockery, but his eyes have a cordial glow. In a pea-gravel bass like the voice of that Cretan singer he says, "It was a good idea. But unfortunately it is not correct." The other three turn toward him. "The word and the name are from different roots. Also, the spelling—in the word, the first *ee* is an *ypsilon*, but in the name, an *ita*."

"Ah," I say. "So there's no connection."

"But it was a good idea."

I thank the man, toast him and ask if he would like to join us, but he says he's about to leave and go home. He doesn't leave. He remains at his table, facing the stove, silently smoking and drinking ouzo, until finally we ourselves depart.

Outside, over the thudding of the oil press and the hyperventilations of the donkeys, I tell the others, "And there's another reason I want to live here."

"Creepy old guys eavesdropping from the next table?" Iphigenia asks. "Guys chain-smoking while you try to eat? I love Greece and Lesvos, OK, but it's better to visit and then go back across the water."

I smile and don't bother elaborating. To see language as little more than a useful instrument is normal, sensible and probably healthier than delving into its secret life: the fossilized strata underlying daily speech, the rhizomatic connections, the mysteries of language speciation, the sonograph of lost time and Eros encoded in the cadences of an ancient poem.

My encounter with the man revives my resentment of the anti-intellectualism that impoverishes discourse back home. In what small-town restaurant in North America would a stranger at the next table—a farmer, a businessman, a mechanic—be willing and able to clarify an obscure etymology, and with gusto and pride? Greece teems with "common people" who know their own language and culture better than most academic specialists in North America know theirs. Which may in fact be the precondition for a living culture: that its knowledge be democratically distributed, not confined to an elite who address mainly each other in a kind of gated dialect.

Another quiet evening in the harbour. On the closed-in front porch of the Captain's Kitchen, eight volunteers crowd around a table. Seven—including Cyrus, Asim, Klea and Pilar—attend to tablets, laptops, mobile phones. I sit writing in my notebook. Despite this collective silence, the moment feels companionable. Down the steps on the pier, other volunteers in scarves, hoodies, parkas and lap blankets cluster around a table watching an episode of *Planet Earth*, David Attenborough hamming it up as usual.

Under a lamp on the pier's edge, the usual congress of pariah cats has gathered: an even twenty tonight, some curled on piles of orange netting or on coils of thick rope that resemble dormant constrictors. Forty feline ears cocked for the drone of boats returning. No motion but for the swish of a tail.

Cyrus nudges me with his elbow and turns his laptop toward me. One of Jack Marvin's photographs fills the screen. A figure lies under a blanket on a pier at night. A few steps from the body, a tall, gaunt volunteer of around my age stands facing away, smoking hard, the steeply falling lamplight skulling his face.

"He seems to hate people," Cyrus says in an undertone, "but he has a heart."

"Who?" I ask stupidly, focused on the death's head of the thin man in the picture, trying to construe his features out of shadow. "Oh—you mean Jack."

"Obviously."

Asim looks up—brown circles under his eyes like those of a much older man—then back down at his device.

When I step outside, I notice the owners of the empty restaurant next door slumped in their doorway, an aproned old man and woman staring out at the dark harbour.

Death to the ferryman

PEOPLE IN A DISASTER ZONE GET ON WITH THEIR DAYS
and nights among the ruins and the graves.

At the south end of the pier, on a tiny black beach
behind the mariners' chapel, a Turkish fishing boat lies on
its beam ends, cross-sectioned and gutted. On its final voyage,
the twenty-eight-foot *Haker*, grossly overladen, was being
"steered" by a novice the human smugglers had randomly
appointed when it collided with a Greek coast guard vessel.
At least thirteen of the passengers were killed in the colli-
sion or drowned afterward. (At first I assumed this was the
October disaster Harry and Lindsay were involved in, but
no, this one happened in August. The wreck already looks
years old.)

Tonight, volunteers are crowded around a bonfire
on this scallop of beach, drinking leftover *glühwein* that

Belinda and Tassos made for the town Christmas Fair and eating bowlfuls of the lentil stew that the wrecked anarchist chefs continue to prepare each night, as if any morning now the refugees will begin landing again. Trapped on the Turkish coast, they might be warming themselves around fires of their own tonight unless they're afraid to light any, what with the Turkish police rounding up hundreds of them, or so we hear.

A cauldron of *glühwein* steams over a camp stove beside the wreck. Volunteers file toward it for refills as the party grows rowdier. Someone has brought out a guitar. A scent of weed eclipses the smells of lemon and cinnamon, spicy lentil stew, cigarettes. Elated young faces in the firelight and, behind them, the rotting cenotaph of the *Haker*... this juxtaposition might seem jarring, the choice of location insensitive. But this is the best place for a fire, nothing can be done about the wreck, and any opportunity for fun and laughter—a few women up dancing now, dangerously close to the flames—is reason enough.

Ratko in his black track suit and toque hulks around like event security, his low voice and thuggish chuckles steadily audible. Jack with his Nikon cameras lurks on the party's penumbra, his brow and lips crimped like a photo-artist forced to work weddings amid bellowing groomsmen and shrieking bridesmaids.

My guest-house neighbour Clara Romero is one of the dancers. The guitarist snaps out Neil Young's "Rockin' in the Free World" and sings in a German-accented falsetto; Clara grips a sloshing mug of *glühwein*, a lit cigarette in her lips as she freestyles among Scandinavians young enough to be her granddaughters. She models that good advice that to dance well means letting a beat infiltrate your hips, not your feet, while using your ass to inscribe your name on the air in cursive letters.

Firelight is a forgiving light, easing and erasing years from a face, but it isn't doing much for the burned-out veterans. They gape into the flames with slack, absent expressions and stupefied eyes. Harry, Lindsay, Danny, this breather, after your months of front-lining—of mainlining the body's own amphetamines—is offering not a deserved respite but simply the leisure to sink into exhaustion and sickness. Omiros is the only veteran who doesn't seem ill; tonight, along with Klaus, Shayn and Astrid, he's holding the fort at OXY, where the huge sleeping tents are empty.

As I line up to refill my mug, Pol, a skinny Swedish biology major, tells me that last month two members of Sweden's white supremacist party were sent down here to hand out leaflets warning arriving refugees that there would be no welcome, no jobs, no homes for them in Sweden. To the consternation of these two and the puzzlement of volunteers, the refugees—alone or gathered around one person reading out the material—were seen grinning, slapping thighs and baying with laughter. Asim picked up a leaflet and found that the Arabic was not only mutilated but comically archaic. He reckoned the Swedes must have used an online site programmed to translate not into modern but into classical Arabic. The effect might have been like reading, *Fare ye not to our pleasant northern Land, ye dusky Peoples of the Prophet, for there shall ye find neither Abode nor wageful Employ!*

Back to the cauldron queue. A young guy in a puffy parka and tiny round spectacles asks where I'm from. He's attached to Drapen i Havet, the Norwegian NGO. I answer him and he says, "I prefer the way *your* country is moving—towards more freedoms, for people like myself."

Does he mean young people? Educated people?

"I am an anarcho-capitalist," he shouts over the noise of the party.

After a moment I say loudly, "You mean a libertarian?"

"Basically, yes!"

I lean in toward his ear and say, "The question I always ask about libertarians is... how come you never meet a poor one?"

"Yes!" he cries.

"What?"

"Yes, exactly!"

"Well, have you?"

"No!"

At midnight the bonfire is at its hottest. Sparks like miniature squibs shoot high and crackle and for a moment complicate and revise the constellations—the big and small dippers, Cygnus, Cassiopeia, its clear W insisting on the coming season. A split of wood tumbles out of the pyre, a dancer jumps over it to screams of laughter, it rolls to a stop on the sand a few feet from Harry. He doesn't move—barely seems to notice. Earlier, Pilar, who has been helping Lindsay with logistics, told me they have just removed Harry from the schedule and he will be returning to Britain tomorrow. Same with Lindsay in a few more days; Pilar has been begging her to go and finally she has agreed.

From somewhere a voice declaims, "They will sail again in great numbers within a few days! This I feel!"

I say good night to Clara, who doesn't aim to leave any time soon and seems scandalized by my departure: "It's not even one, Stavro!"

"Seven a.m. shift at Efthalou." I clink her mug and offer the local toast that has become my default, *"Na pethanei o Xaros!"*—*Death to the ferryman*, or *Death to Death*—as if the wreckage looming behind the dancers could be His vessel, beached and gutted, never to set out again.

Tannenbaum

AS THE BLOCKADE DRAGS ON, THE SENSE OF INERTIA and waning initiative deepens. Tonight we try to keep ourselves engaged, and warm, by helping to decorate the camp for Christmas. Two of the Green Helmets—carpenters attached to a small German NGO that sends its volunteers to crisis zones—have hammered together a Tannenbaum like an immense, party-sized coat tree. Larry, Iphigenia and I are festooning it with ribbons, bulbs and baubles from a Mithymna shop, and paper angels made by local schoolchildren. Someone has downloaded a playlist of holiday crooner songs, Elvis Presley now lamenting his blue, blue Christmas.

"A Jew helping decorate a Christmas tree made by Germans for the benefit of Muslims," Larry says. "Retirement does open a world of possibilities."

"I feel this is right," Omiros calls down—he's up on a stool, trying to fit a patriarchal sock puppet (Joseph, or a prematurely greying Jesus) onto the wedge of wood that forms the tree's apex—"because where they are going, this is the winter holiday they will see. So this is a sooner welcome to their new life."

Kanella lies on her side snoring beside a brightly painted cardboard-box playhouse that Astrid and Clara crafted this morning. The dog looks overfed. Then I notice her nipples protruding through the short fur of her swollen belly—a miracle, it seems, in keeping with the season! Since making the camp her home she has fiercely vetoed—or so we believed—all canine violations of her perimeter, even running off Larry's gangling, bashful hound, Chet.

I kneel down to scratch her ears. She purrs like a house cat. A flash of red catches my eye: in the shelter doorway, Pericles in a Santa Claus hat has just toppled a Green Helmet with a foot sweep. Now he reaches down, clasps the young man's hand and heaves him to his feet.

"I thought you were saving your best moves for me," I call to him.

"I have many moves, Stavro. The night shift is long."

The Green Helmets have also built an arm wrestling table, complete with dowel counter-grips; says one of them, "We must think too of the energies of young men." Now, as Omiros steps down off the stool, still holding the bearded puppet ("Maybe an angel instead, Stavro? This doll looks too much like an authority figure"), a tournament breaks out. Pericles crushes a young Green Helmet and then, veins swelling in his neck and temples, concedes a long round to Omiros. Seeing my chance, I challenge the flushed, fatigued

Omiros and hold him for a minute or two. When he wins, Iphigenia gives us all a facetious ovation.

Now Pericles nods toward Omiros and says to me, "You see, Stavro—the arms of Homer have very strong mice!"

"Pardon?"

Omiros looks mystified—probably thinks he has misheard.

"I think he must mean 'muscle,'" Iphigenia says. "Don't you, Pericles? In Greek, they're almost the same—mouse, muscle."

"*Mousle,*" Pericles enunciates happily.

"Stavro, you are stronger than I thought," says Omiros, "for a thin man who is almost old. I will need your thinness and your muscle, soon. Thinness, because we must ride together on my small scooter. Muscle, because we will go to Skala, to take back a generator that Antifa will not return."

Staying alive

JUST AFTER SUNRISE, WORD COMES THAT TWO BOATS have slipped through the blockade. Half an hour later two buses arrive at OXY and some sixty Syrians briskly emerge from one, fifty or so Kurds from the other. They look to be in decent shape. After the rush ends at the clothing tent and canteen, I'm standing outside in the sunlight with Kanella to warm up, when two young men approach. Both wear nice if rumpled blazers, designer jeans soaked from the knees down, battered dress shoes. The shoes appear to be from the shoe tent, but clearly the men decided not to trade down for drier clothes. Kanella retreats toward the canteen hut as they approach. The short, sturdy, intense-looking one strides ahead of his chubby companion, whose face is sweat-glazed despite the chill in the air.

"You haven't any coffee," the first one says. It sounds like an annoyed accusation but then he adds quickly, in schooled-sounding English, "Is there somewhere we can find coffee?"

I point back over my shoulder. "You went past it on the bus, just back there along the highway. I'll walk over with you."

"Yes, friend—come with us and we will buy you a coffee."

"How about if I buy them? Your day started a lot earlier than mine."

He scowls with what little forehead he has (his tight-curled hair, seemingly gelled, starts close above his heavy eyebrows), then gets my meaning: "Ah. Yes. Our day began sixty hours ago. I am Sulaiman. The coffee is on us."

"Steve." We shake hands.

"My colleague, he speaks English also. We are working together in Damascus."

"Steve," I repeat, offering my hand to the unnamed friend, who gives it a damp, flaccid shake and says nothing. He too has gelled hair, gold neck bling and an aeronautical wristwatch; he smiles with well-tended teeth.

We cross the highway and walk along the guardrail toward the lookout pull-off where an enterprising local has parked a canteen truck and serves coffee, tea and pastries (OXY is still awaiting delivery of two institutional-sized urns for hot drinks). Sulaiman relates their story while his friend—out of breath but smiling—listens and nods on cue. They were working at a French bank in Damascus, very good jobs, very well paid. Only a week ago they had both been promoted. Most younger men had already been drafted into Assad's army, but they were immune because Sulaiman's uncle had important connections. "Anyway, we believed we had such immunity. But three days ago, we received the draft letters. This duty is a death sentence." Sulaiman again scowls with his drastic eyebrows, as if expecting me to debate the point, while his friend nods and smiles agreeably.

"This was just three days ago?"

"We left at midnight that night. We took our money, no possessions, and left. I had such beautiful clothes there, and shoes!" His friend raises his eyebrows for emphasis: *such shoes*!

"What kind of coffee, my friend?" Sulaiman asks me.

"Double espresso. Let me get it."

"We will hear nothing of this! Please, we have a lot of money."

"They have a lot of money," echoes the Greek proprietor with an ambiguous leer, looking down at us from his wicket. Grey brush-cut hair and the shaggy moustache of a sheep-stealing outlaw.

"Not all of them," I say.

"Oh, we sympathize!" the Greek bursts out as if the Syrians are not standing right there—as if he hasn't just heard one of them speak English. "We hope the best for them! But another summer so quiet, no tourists? Mithymna will die!" He turns to Sulaiman and his colleague: "For you, my friends?"

Sulaiman replies brusquely: "Two coffees."

The Greek nods coolly, turns back to me and says, louder again: "For now, we have the volunteers here, the NGO people, even some refugees who buy my coffee and

food. But when they leave, will the tourists return? We
will see!"

Sulaiman selects a bill from a mahogany-coloured wal-
let and tells the Greek to keep the change.

As we walk back down the shoulder of the road, holding our paper cups, the camp sound system starts playing
Leonard Cohen. I can't make out the words from here but I
know what they are. The war is finished, the good guys lost.

"You know he's Canadian?" I ask. "A lot of folks think
he's American."

"I think he is a Jew," Sulaiman says, his friend nodding
as if happily confirming the fact. I wait uneasily. Sulaiman
growls, "And he is a great singer."

"Well, he might dispute that."

"Is he still alive?"

"Very much so." I lift my paper cup. "Death to the ferryman, Leonard."

They were able to get here in just sixty hours, Sulaiman
says, because of their money. They purchased a kind of
express package from the human smugglers and travelled
by car out of Syria before flying from southeastern Turkey
to Izmir. They booked into an Izmir hotel last night. At 2
a.m., the human smugglers roused them and took them by
taxi to the shore. At 4 a.m. they were instructed to squeeze
aboard a rubber raft with sixty strangers; at this final stage,
apparently, there was to be no special treatment, no reduc-
tion of risks. Sulaiman had complained that the smugglers
were violating their contract. They said, "Get in the boat
if you want to cross."

They crossed without incident and without taking on
much water.

"What about the blockade?" I ask. "Did you see any Turkish ships?"

"Yes, and they had searchlights. I think they must have seen us but they did nothing. I am not sure why. If we could have bribed the Turkish navy, we would have, but of course we did not. Maybe they are simply tired."

In the camp we walk past some older men sitting on pink plastic milk crates around a table freshly built by the Green Helmets. On it, dozens of euro banknotes of modest denomination are drying in the sun, one end of each paper-weighted with a stone, the other rippling in the breeze. Two men have removed shabby suit jackets and one of them is slitting a lapel with a razor blade, the other drawing bills out of a hole he must have cut just now in the hem under the pocket. Sulaiman glances over, then averts his darkening gaze. Is it the men's undisguised poverty? Does he feel they're embarrassing Syria? Is he embarrassed—even slightly, momentarily—at his own wealth? He's one of the first fluent English speakers I've met among the refugees, yet I'm no closer to knowing him than knowing any of the others.

Returning in late afternoon, I decide to climb on past the guest house and finally visit the Crusader castle high above the town. The going is steep and hot. Though the shortest day of the year is barely a week from now, this light-condensing labyrinth of alleys turns the season back into midsummer.

Siesta: all windows shuttered, doors shut, the town silent as a dream. I round a corner exposed to the north—terracotta rooftops falling away to a distant harbour, tiny boats—and meet one of the town's countless stray cats, a small tortoiseshell. At first I think there's a bloodied mouse clamped in its teeth. I step closer. No, it's the cat's nose, its whole muzzle torn or bitten off, a pulpy violet mess. It doesn't cry but looks up at me with eyes that seem bewildered, beseeching. Finally it meows weakly. I'm surprised it can make any sound. Are there teeth left in there? The wound is clotted but not yet scabbing. I kneel down, reach out and murmur what I hope are soothing sounds. Its remaining face twitches and a few unshattered fangs show amid the gore. A muffled hiss. My hand recoils.

I stand up, stare down. After a few seconds, I walk on up the lane. The cat has no home and I don't see how I can pick it up and I wouldn't know where to take it. No veterinarian in a town aswarm with strays will take in one damaged, maybe dying, cat. Yet as I climb higher my conscience prods me.

My thoughts are paused by a second apparition, hobbling ahead of me, an ancient, shrivelled man barely four feet tall, each palsied arm braced in a sleeved aluminum cane. The rest of the town has succumbed to the urge to rest, yet he, who must be closer to eternal rest than any of them, resists, halting along through these white canyons as if to hold off sleep, or outpace it. How is he managing these broken pavestones and potholes? Hesitant to pass him, I hold back and watch as he creaks on around a turning in the lane. By the time I round the turn he's gone, swallowed by one of the unnumbered doors along this last stretch before the peak.

That evening at the Alonia, when I describe my meeting with the cat, a new volunteer from Belgium says, "If you will come here to help human strangers, why not this poor cat who suffers so?" I glance at her plate of pork souvlaki, considering a response. Then it strikes me—if someone had told a story similar but involving a dog, I might have reacted as this woman has and thought nothing of what's on my own plate: a "vegetarian boureki" oozing cheese made from the milk of a cow whose calf was taken away and slaughtered so we could harvest the milk.

I wake at dawn after watching a man who is me but doesn't look it—younger by some years and yet white-haired—astride a corpse performing chest compressions, on and on, *over an hour already*, a voice says, *you should stop now*, and the one who is me and isn't me is weeping as he keeps on pumping. *You must do it in time to the song!* yells another voice, Slavic accent. *Which song?* I ask the voices. No one can remember which song. And the corpse is rapidly shrinking, the grey skin morphing into the latex integument of a medical dummy.

A pillow for the crossing

ALL QUIET AGAIN ON EFTHALOU BEACH. THE RISING sun is already warm and the sea unperturbed—ideal conditions for a crossing, were it not for the blockade. Oddly, only a single Turkish ship is in view now. Where have the others gone? I leave Klaus beside the fire in the morning sunshine, telling him I'm going to have a look from up on the cliffs.

I hike east up the dirt road that leads toward Skala: a steeply climbing and dipping track too rutted and narrow for buses. Tens of thousands of refugees have walked this road since the spring, though they've been coming west, toward Efthalou, from whatever cove they've beached in. In either direction the going is tough, even for someone who spent the night in a bed and started the day with Greek coffee, figs, pistachios, warm bread dunked in cold-pressed oil.

From the edge of an arc in the road, I look way down into a cove where an abandoned dinghy lies beached, toylike at this drone's-eye distance. To climb up to where I am, the passengers, likely including children, must have scaled the loose, eroding bluffs below the road.

On a headland across the way, a white van is parked, *MSF* inscribed on it in crimson caps. It's not a hundred metres off as the crow flies but much farther on foot, the road curving inland along a ravine before looping back out to the cape. As I follow the road, I find myself singing, then singing louder—the ravine is a miraculous resonator—and the song welling out of me is, for whatever reason, Gillian Welch's "Miner's Refrain." This spontaneous paean might be a yawp of raw gratitude for the flowing ease and freedom of my limbs today, this light, this view of the sea and the far coast widening as I climb on. *I'm down in a hole, way down in a deep dark hole...* Of all the things to sing, here and now! Lines about the debt peonage of Appalachian coal miners—like the debt serfdom of Greece—and about the pit of sadness that can gape under any psyche, any time. All the more reason never to ignore pulses of pure elation, if and when they come, as now for a man suspended between lives, the old and the emerging, unrevealed. All the more reason for anybody as the world's mood, overtaken by the dusk, darkens. The fiddler at a wake doesn't apologize for reeling off "Whiskey in the Jar" beside the open coffin near dawn.

The blond-bearded Viking manning the Médecins Sans Frontières lookout tells me he is grateful for my singing—not, it turns out, because he thought it was any good but because he'd dozed off in his seat facing out to sea and my echoing voice woke him. His seat: a Hollywood director's chair with *MSF* stencilled on the canvas back panel. "I am replacing an ill watchman. I was in Moria last night till five in the morning. I must stay awake now some way, ha!"

"It must be hard with no boats crossing."

"But they are trying to come! At dawn I saw several launch out." He indicates the long-scoped green binoculars hanging around his neck. "But a Turkish ship—that only one that you see there?—it made them turn back. The sailormen shot a water cannon. They filled a raft with water and the jet knocked people into the sea, but they could all climb back in. So, happy ending! But they made the raft turn back."

Before I can respond he rushes on: "You can imagine how I felt, watching this alone! I was talking to myself, then I was *yelling*, maybe louder than your song. You would like hot coffee, maybe? I'll make us good coffee in the truck. I am doing some yoga to stay awake, ha, but now strong coffee, good company, so I can talk to some person who is not myself…"

I tell him I really should head back down.

Ten minutes later I look back across the ravine and the big Norwegian waves, his grin visible from here. His lookout post and directorial chair call to mind a passage that has stuck with me from Herodotus's *The Histories*, which I read maybe a quarter century ago. The Persian king, Xerxes, is invading Greece with a horde like a locust swarm—well over a million men, according to Herodotus. The king wishes to survey his army-and-navy in its gratifying entirety, so on a mountain overlooking the plain and the sea he has a dais of white stone constructed from which he can inspect his force—this prodigious extension of himself—as it pushes into Greece. But while reviewing the world's largest-ever military parade, the commander-in-chief begins to weep. When one of his entourage inquires why, Xerxes says compassion overcame him at the realization that, out of this invincible multitude, not a single man would be left alive in a century.

Where the road swoops down to sea level and Efthalou Beach, I veer right onto a lane that leads, I've been told, to a nineteenth-century Ottoman bathhouse fed by a hot spring. I soon reach it. It resembles a large stucco igloo. Behind it, cliffs tower, shadowing the narrow, stony beach. The bathhouse door is padlocked, mist escaping from vents in the side. Next to the dome, a large, shuttered stone house, reputedly an old spa hotel, now abandoned.

Behind the bath dome, at ground level, an outlet like a mouse hole. Water gurgles steadily from the hole, steam hovers above it. It rills down across the shingle to form a small pool among the seaside boulders. I take off my boots and socks, then roll up my jeans to soak my feet and calves in the pool. It has been days since I've felt hot water. Beautiful. I decide to make a bathtub among the boulders. I remove jeans and jacket, hunker deep in the cavity and lift rocks out of the bottom and from along the sides. Having dredged and widened the pool as much as possible—taken it down to bedrock, its walls immovable boulders—I strip fully and get in. The water smells mineralized but unsulphurous. The hollow is large enough that I can lie back, immersed to my sternum, my knees exposed. Hot water pulses against the small of my back; at my feet, every minute or so, seawater wells in through a gap between boulders, keeping this paleolithic hot tub from overheating.

There's a splash from in front of the stone house. I sit up and look: just ripples on the sea's surface. Then the face of a woman bobs up. She is breaststroking straight out in the direction of the sunlit Turkish coast. From where I sit, she looks middle-aged, darkly tan, her gold hair bunned. Where has she come from? Now I see that a door and the shutters of one of the old spa's rooms—a few steps from the sea across a hem of pebble beach—are open, a towel draped over the windowsill. The woman strokes out to the edge of the cliff shadow, then turns and in the sunlight cruises back and forth, parallel to shore, like those ships blockading the far coast. Or, today, that single ship.

Oddly, I can't see even that one ship now.

A breeze starts up, the swell rises. Every eighth or ninth swell pumps the pool full of freezing water, which then drains out while hot water seeps back in, re-warming it. It's exhilarating, the latest of the day's gifts. But within minutes the swells are swamping me, tossing me around. A thermal dispute that seemed evenly matched has become a rout. I need to get out but don't want to startle the woman, who is now swimming back into the cove.

She stands up in the shallows, a sun-leathered, starved-looking person of around eighty, in a string bikini. Her hair must be dyed. Her skin has the unnatural walnut stain of a north European who has spent many years in a sunny climate. Seeing my face among the steaming rocks, she gives a curt, incurious wave, as if my presence here is neither surprising nor interesting. She steps onto the pebbles, pulls her white towel from the windowsill and shrouds her bones, then pads inside like the spectral last patient haunting a shuttered sanatorium.

I leap out and reach for my clothes—mostly wet. As I dress, I glimpse something out in the channel and straighten up and refocus: sunlight glinting off a number of dark, rounded snouts, like a pod of whales ploughing shoreward. The fleet of dinghies seem to be bearing to the east of here—not Efthalou Beach—but they will be landing soon, after which their passengers will be tramping west along the road I just walked, past the MSF lookout and down to the beach.

Off Efthalou Beach a fishing boat quietly plies its trade, as if unaware of the rafts approaching the island like landing craft. Of course the crew is aware. They're just getting on with their work, as they and their kind have done in the midst of crisis for several thousand years. Larry, who has joined Klaus by the fire, says rafts have already begun to land farther up the coast and as many as six hundred refugees could be on their way. Other volunteers have come down from the atelier and now Delilah, in her action-figure wetsuit, pulls up on the Housmans' scooter.

"I thought you were on Xios, with Drop in the Ocean?" I yell over the two-stroke motor's gunning.

"They kicked us off!"

"Off the island? Why... how?"

"Logistical differences. Strategic disagreements."

"Like what?"

"Like the island was their personal domain or something! Whatever. The refugees are landing here again."

She peels away up the dirt road toward Skala.

I drop to one knee in the sand and help Larry and Klaus build up the bonfire. Larry sits spraddle-legged on a canvas camp stool, Klaus hunkers over his bare feet like a sadhu. Each life vest we toss onto the fire has been slit open where a volunteer checked if it was real, hence burnable.

"Were many the genuine article today?" I ask.

Swiping his brow with a handkerchief, Larry says: "Maybe the coyotes are feeling sensitive about all the bad press, huh? Most of the ones I cut open this morning were real."

"Or, we see a small contagion of morality," Klaus says, barely audible. "I fear it passes like a cough."

We check and count our different-coloured tickets for the buses and then organize the loading zone, using ropes and wooden posts on cruciform stands to create a safe lane along the beach side of the road. Back beyond the fire, Hayley, a Waldorf grade school teacher from London, is prepping her dry-clothing depot: a medium-sized green military tent. Like a nun raking pebbles in a Zen garden she works with silent pertinacity. She and Delilah could be each other's antimatter: both tall and high-cheekboned, yet one is dark, the other blond, one calmly melancholic, the other noisily flamboyant, one patient, the other impulsive, one choosing a support role in the wings, the other eating the mic. But if Delilah's American dynamism is easy to mock, it's also hard to replace.

The first few dozen refugees—those too ill or old to walk—arrive in cars and a few vans small enough for the dirt road. But they don't stop here. The drivers, attached to MSF or the Hellenic Red Cross, slow and wave as they bypass our loading zone, then accelerate up the road toward OXY.

A half-hour later the first walkers appear, silhouetted on the heights above the beach, a few, then dozens, then hundreds flowing over the top and down the dirt road toward us. They're coming surprisingly fast, like competitors in a long road race entering the home stretch, we the finish-line marshals. Their prompt arrival and businesslike queuing-up allay my fears that the blockade and their cold, crowded wait on the other shore might have weakened them dangerously. Many look wet and chilled but their faces and postures radiate relief, even joy.

Twenty minutes later I'm holding a rope across the front of the bus lane, my other hand raised to signal *soon!*, when Delilah zooms up on the scooter and shouts, "Almost ready!" Still in her wetsuit, she points back at the bus idling fifty metres up the road (she has raced over from there). Her face is flushed, eyes flashing: "OK—I'll stay here for a sec! You go back along the line and recount to make sure!"

"Got it," I say, tipping my hat brim. I walk beside the line, pointing and counting out loud for clarity, punctuating my tally with nodding smiles as if otherwise these folks might feel numeralized: penned cattle. But they understand what I'm doing and they help me, raising hands, counting along in Arabic. As I near the limit, sixty, I stop: a man with a large, craggy head and curly hair looms over the others and beams at me as if we're old friends—the very image of the American actor John C. Reilly.

Number sixty is a young man with a confidently handsome brown face. Tricolour Bob Marley sweatshirt, new jeans wet from the knees down, flip-flops. "What's up, friend?" he says.

"You speak English?"

"Sure, of course."

"I haven't met many who do."

"They're Syrians, Kurdish, Afghans. I'm from Gaza."

His dreadlocks are gathered in a Rastafarian bun. In his soft but full black beard, the light sets off a solitary white hair. Before I can ask anything he says, "So at dawn they tell us—seventy of us, mainly Syrians?—they tell us, Carry your boat down this cliff." (I assume he means a rocky slope.) "It was way too heavy, friend." (I nod; I've helped to move beached dinghies; with their engines on, they must weigh half a ton.) "So on this cliff the rocks cut holes through the floor. So the smugglers, they cover the holes with some kind of tape. Yeah, really—tape! Then, they pick somebody to steer the boat and it's me—OK, whatever, I guess 'cause I grew up beside the sea. But I never pirated a boat." After a moment I realize: *piloted*. "Making me steer their shitty boat after I save for like two years to pay for the trip! We pail out water the whole way and the engine quits working like maybe five times."

I tell him it sounds terrifying.

"Not so much for me." Cocky smile, good teeth. I keep looking at that lone, very white beard-hair. "I can swim, man. I'm a great swimmer. I grew up in Gaza. These others here, they were scared shitless. A lot of these people, the men too, they were crying the whole way."

"Can't blame them," says Larry, suddenly beside me in his painter's beret. "But they look all right now."

"Finish counting!" Delilah roars from the front of the line.

"Plus maybe they're scared about crossing borders," the Palestinian adds. "Me, I should be the scared one—no passport!"

"You're serious?"

He shrugs with that carny's grin. "I'll figure it out, man. I'm living my whole life under bombs in a war zone. Like I'm going to be scared of crossing some water and a few fences."

"Looks like we're starting to board," Larry says.

"Be well, friend," the guy tells me, and as we shake hands I feel warm sweat glazing his palm.

All day long they continue to come, maybe seven or eight hundred by late afternoon. The hours surge and blur together. I lose count of the buses. Larry gets slower and grumpier but never quits. Some jolly, industrious Czechs materialize and pitch in. Delilah is omnipresent on her scooter, airlifting things down from the atelier, bossily reorganizing queues, confiscating bags from startled refugees and heaving them into the holds; methed on adrenalin. Meanwhile Hayley has been serving steadily in her tent. When she finishes, she walks over and, without a word, like a good-hearted ghost, slots herself into our team as we finish.

As I walk back to town, the sun is setting behind the castle high on its romantic roost: picturesque, as usual, to the point of satire. To the south looms another sunlit prominence, now large enough to be seen from here and quite possibly from outer space: a vast orange pyramid of tens of thousands of discarded life vests.

When I reach the Alonia I stop in for a drink. Larry is smoking a pipe by the woodstove with Iphigenia and the young Czechs. On their table, a brass jug and small juice glasses full of pale young wine. A young Swiss German named Martin sits with them. He arrived today on the ferry from Samos, having heard rumours—"gossips," he calls them—that the refugees have started crossing again to Lesvos, the shorter, less perilous route.

"Yup, OXY was full when I left just now," Iphigenia says. "Omiros wants people to stay over, for a rest—you know how he is—but the buses keep taking them down to Moria."

"I think the NGOs are plotting to shut us down," Larry says. "There are rumours."

Rumours and gossips, the pistons of discourse in a crisis zone.

Martin's platinum hair is combed straight back from a high widow's peak over pellucid blue eyes. He has a terrifyingly virtuous aspect and yet he's drunk, has been drinking all the day, he says, on the ferry and then here: "I think several litres of the wine, my God!—pardon me." He seems not boastful but surprised: "I am not a normal drunker—normal for me is one beer!"

"Tell Steve your story, Marty," says Larry. "Steve's an author." Martin's gaze is blank, unblinking. He doesn't recognize the word "author," I think, but before I can explain he begins blurting his story, compelled, it seems, like Coleridge's Ancient Mariner. But Martin's tale is simple and brief. He took part in a work detail two days ago on Samos, digging graves for three men who had washed ashore and could not be identified. Having arrived as a novice volunteer just days before that, he had not yet encountered the fake life vest phenomenon. It shocked him; it continues to shock him. His incredulity that people would risk drowning others, some of them children, so as to realize a puny profit is old-fashioned in a touching, no, a moving way. He has been sponsored and sent here by a rural Swiss Lutheran church where he heads the youth group.

"We put the orange vests under their heads. In the, in the box they go in."

"The coffin," Larry says.

"Like a pillow, under the head. There is nothing else to put with them. I want to say a prayer, but of course it would be Christian, so I say nothing." Martin drains his glass again. "But when we fill the holes, I say it quietly."

I will forget his words in the busy days and nights to come, but in time the images will resurface, translated into lines bearing witness to events I never witnessed, like the counter-transference by which therapists can take on the dreams of traumatized patients.

CHRISTMAS WORK DETAIL, SAMOS

Eid milad majid *

In the olive grove on the high ground, facing west
into rain, we dig graves for three men drowned
in the straits—Syrians, maybe, dispossessed
of everything by the sea, so there's no knowing

for sure. This much you can say for any grave,
it's landlocked. And these men will lie a decent
distance uphill, out of sight of the beach
where on Sunday their bodies washed ashore

in plausible orange life vests (ten euros each)
packed with sawdust, bubble wrap, rags. These rains
haven't softened the soil, yet digging up here
feels only right; the waves that buried them

terrified them first, and we guess, again,
that they—like the ones the crossing didn't kill—
were from desert towns, this sea inconceivable
as the Arctic. And each cardboard casket,

awaiting its patient passenger, looks
almost seaworthy after the cut-rate raft
they fled in, and which, deflated, washed in
later in silence, as if shyly contrite.

It seems we've failed them, despite the safe graves.
In a grove this untended the ground is brined
bitter with black fruit rotting, and on islands
nowhere is far enough from the waves.

* Arabic for *Happy birth feast*, or *Merry Christmas*

3. INTENSIFICATION

DECEMBER 21, 2015, MYTILENE, LESVOS: *In the wake of yesterday's riot in Camp Moria, the main refugee centre on Lesvos, volunteer organizations on the island have put out a collective call for help. According to Belinda Grivakes of the Captain's Kitchen, a volunteer foundation based in Mithymna (or Molyvos), many volunteers are leaving, either because of exhaustion or for the Christmas holidays. "But refugees won't stop risking their lives to come here," Grivakes said. "Over the last week, the numbers have been growing again. We need more hands. Above all, we need more help and aid with infrastructure. The situation, especially in Moria, is desperate." Grivakes added that, while the official estimate of refugees who have crossed the channel between Turkey and Lesvos in 2015 is now 500,000, the actual number is far higher.*

* * *

They'd chased after the hope of a more dignified life...
Once we'd stripped the bodies, we began our inspection.

—*Davide Enia*, Notes on a Shipwreck, *tr. Antony Shugaar*

Over the mountains to Skala

AS SODDEN REFUGEES STREAM BACK INTO OXY AND the weather turns harsher, Omiros insists that retrieving the camp's lost generator is urgent. Back in October he borrowed it from the Red Cross and then re-lent it to Antifa, who were trying to expand their own camp at Skala Sykamineas. Now Antifa keeps ignoring his requests to return it. Omiros does not love the Red Cross but has promised to give the generator back to them, and he is a man of his word, he says, except sometimes when it comes to sex and love, but then what lover always keeps every promise? He adds further that if we do retrieve it, he might not return it immediately, since at OXY we're still waiting for another backup generator to arrive.

I wait for him at the bus stop on the edge of town. He rattles up on a rented Vespa—a tall and dignified man straddling what looks like a child's toy, dinged and dirty, the little back tire almost flat. He wears wraparound shades like re-entry shields. His huge white helmet, one of the few I've seen on anyone in Greece, gives him an extraterrestrially large head. "Here, Stavro. One for you too." Another helmet. Inserting a cigarette in his mouth he says, "This expedition could be dangerous."

"The mountain roads, or reclaiming the generator?"

He simply nods.

"And I'm supposed to be your hired goon?"

"Pardon?"

"Your enforcer."

"Yes, enforcer! We will both be enforcers! And while we are in Skala, we can have a salad."

Despite the impeccable timing, I see no sign that he is kidding.

After re-inflating our go-kart tires and refuelling, we ride inland, taking the paved route over the mountains instead of the washed-out dirt road along the coast. I expect us to pass through a gauntlet of grins induced by the spectacle of two men, maybe three hundred and fifty pounds together, in bulbous helmets, crammed on a scooter like a couple of circus bears. But our route seems deserted. The day is cool, overcast, a mournful Sunday quiescence shrouding the land.

"Where will we fit the generator when we ride back?" I yell.

"The generator?" Omiros calls back. "Who knows if it will fit?"

The road hairpins up into the mountains and soon we're in empty autumnal country, yellow leaves falling from the ancient oaks, the cold air smelling of leaf fires. Across the straits the mountains of Asia Minor recede wave by wave, the farther ranges powdered with snow. On the downhill stretches Omiros opens the throttle and for thrilling moments we soar as if on a real bike.

The road descending the cliffs at Skala is, as the name itself forewarns, steep as a stairway. We brake-pump down the switchbacks, at moments almost toppling over the handlebars as the creaking brake pads scorch. At the bottom we glide through the silent village, then follow the coast road along the wreck-strewn beach to the Seventh-day Adventist medi-van and the row of tents and huts facing the sea, where I first saw refugees come ashore.

Today the camp has the air of an evacuated shantytown. We dismount and approach the one visible being, a pinched, weathered woman who stands behind a table, stirring a fuming cauldron under a snapping flag: *ANTIFA* inscribed over a background of anarchist black and communist red. She has dark hair striated with white and tugged back in a bun, dark shawls and scarves layered but barely padding the lattice of her frail frame. She ignores us, stirring—the pot's contents smell like sweet, milky tea—until we reach the table.

She sets down the long ladle and faces us.

"*Me synchoreite*," I say—she looks Greek—"*Vriskoume*—"

"What do you want?" she interrupts in English with a Greek accent. "You would like some tea? There's plenty." She claps a couple of nested Styrofoam cups on the table.

Omiros sets his helmet down beside the cups and then takes them up with grave ceremony, as if receiving the Grail. "I thank you." Looking feelingly at the woman he says, "We are here to take back a generator we have let you use. I must return it to the Red Cross."

"As if they need it!"

Her smile is livid, deep lines parenthesizing her mouth.

"But I have promised," he says. "And I have called to ask you before."

"You make a promise to let a rich organization take our generator?"

"It is theirs," he says gently. He seems unruffled, while I'm bracing for a confrontation, shivering, chilled from the ride. I feared this errand might be harder than he expected.

"They let me use it at a time when we had nothing at OXY," he says.

"OXY? So you must be the famous Omiros."

"And this is Steven." He says it in the Spanish way, E*stay*ban. He hands me a Styrofoam cup. "He is one of the volunteers for Captain's Kitchen."

"The Captain's Kitchen!" She bares her grey teeth again.

"So, you see, I must return the generator."

"And if it's our only one? Last night we had twenty refugees with us."

"It is not your only one. I have confirmed this fact."

"And if the other one stops working?"

"For us, the situation is the same."

"Let the Red Cross come to us itself!"

"If I break my promise, why would they help me again next week?"

Full stop. They stare at each other. Finally she extends her hand, as if demanding the cup back. He passes it to her and she ladles it full of the steaming, caramel-brown tea. She gives me a curt nod and I hand her my cup. I thank her in Greek and sip the hot, sweet tea; in English she asks me if I'm Spanish.

"I want to say this to you"—Omiros frowning solemnly, holding his cup but still not drinking—"I am very grateful to you for helping my people here."

The woman shrugs, stirring the cauldron with the ladle. "It seems little enough. You are Syrian yourself, yes, they told me so."

"My father was Syrian. I believe people like you do more for the refugees, and with less money, than the NGOs ever do."

"Less money? No money!"

"And now I believe they want to close us—OXY—and take control of everything. I think they will try to do it to you also."

"They are trying," she says with another grimace. "Let them try!"

"But I must have that generator."

A huge, hairy man ducks out of a nearby tent with a cigarette protruding from his beard. The beard rises almost to his eyes. Thick curly hair begins just above his wild eyebrows. He blurts something in Greek, the woman snaps a reply, I get only a couple of words. I stand up straighter, clutching my helmet under my arm.

"And so, Omiros refuses to depart otherwise," the woman says through that furious smile. I peer closer; under her layers she seems even thinner now, as if years of rage at injustice have burned her away and left just sinew, bone and will. Antifa's mandate is to fight fascism not just with words and worthy intentions but toe to toe in the street. Backing up beliefs and slogans with risky action merits respect, maybe sympathy, too, since enlisting rage as a daily fuel levies such a toll on the mind and body.

"I'm sorry?" he asks.

"Not depart without his generator!"

"Ah, yes, exactly."

Another exchange between her and the wolfman and then he beckons us to follow him in among the tents and sheds. He pulls aside a flap. We duck into a dim tent that instantly fills with his cigarette smoke. "*Oriste*," he says mildly, pointing. The generator is propping up a pile of split wood. Two axes and a mallet lean against its other flank. It's not much bigger than a carry-on bag. As the object of an inquiry, a two-man quest and now an argument between allies, it seems puny and unprepossessing. We've entered the mode of the mock-heroic. Still, when I heft the thing, I discover it's far more substantial than it appears, weighing maybe a hundred pounds.

We thank the woman, who now seems resigned to turning over the idle generator, maybe even a little pleased. She offers a refill of tea and tells Omiros, "Perhaps we will work together in the future. Captain's Kitchen is not the place for you."

Noncommittally he inclines his head: "I hope we will see each other again."

Behind a restaurant in the village, among empty tables near the deserted pier, Omiros rolls a hash joint and we smoke it and drink green tea. He doesn't touch alcohol, he says, and the chill in my bones is such that a hot drink is all I crave. A waiter has brought out not sugar but honey and, as I put a spoonful in my tea, Omiros says, "That much is the lifetime work of just one bee. Honey is good, but this is a tragedy."

A welter of squawking and honking emerges from the restaurant. When we finish our tea, we go to investigate. Near the back door a pastel-coloured papagallo roosts on a wooden high chair, nattering in Greek. Omiros and I stand staring at the bird while it orates, louder now, invigorated by this audience of two glassy-eyed men.

"Will you interpret this speech for me, Stavro?"

I cock my ear. After some moments I realize the bird has exhausted its repertoire and is repeating itself, though artfully, varying its cadences and adding a lisp.

"I love you in the moonlight," I translate. "I sing for you like Sappho."

I thing for you like Thappho.

I step closer and put out my hand. An aproned woman with a black-dyed beehive approaches, eyeing us over her bifocals. "*Prosekhe,*" she says, a warning—though her manner is utterly indifferent.

"Oh—he bites?" I ask with hash-numbed lips.

"Certainly he bites!" She splays her hands as if nothing could be more obvious, nor less worrisome to her. Whatever Greek business owners fear these days—and on Lesvos, abandoned by the tourists, there is much to fear—injury lawsuits are not among them.

As I notice the lacquered tree trunk thirty feet behind her, I realize which restaurant we're in: Life in the Grave, as on my first night in Skala. I ask her to seat us beside the great trunk, which would have been alive and unenclosed in 1923 when Stratis Myrivilis sat writing under its canopy and Greek refugees from Turkey continued to arrive at the pier, boat after boat, and herd past his table.

We order food: the salad that Omiros improbably proposed earlier, along with stewed wild greens glistening with oil and lemon juice and little gemstones of rock salt, tarama-salata, bread, and grilled *barbounia* caught this morning. So Omiros is not a vegetarian as I'd assumed after his remark about honeybees.

I order myself a half-litre of the dry rosé from Xios. When it arrives, I hold the carafe up to the firelight: stained-glass ruby with cochineal depths. I explain to Omiros that where I come from, many men avoid drinking rosé, at least in public, because of its pinkness. He looks mystified. I can't tell whether my meaning was unclear or if he simply finds the meaning bizarre. He says, "Why will they do this thing? It is stupid. This colour... it is the colour of a woman's lips..."

Now he explains that he had "a serious thing" with one of the volunteer women last fall, before he had to go back to Spain. "When I returned here," he adds, "she felt it would start again, but no, I found others. Sadly."

"Others?"

"I meant another."

He had gone back to Spain, he says, because his mother was very ill. As for his Syrian father, he can barely remember the man's face now. He toothpicks a fishbone out of his molars and sets it on the rim of his plate among sucked olive pits.

I'm failing to sip the wine. It comes into my head to say, *You came here for your father, didn't you? As if to meet him on the beaches.* Of course I'm not going to say that. But while the thought is still loose in my head, *he* asks, "If your mother is not Greek, would you be here with us on Lesvos?"

"I don't know," I say quickly. "Probably not."

"I see."

"'Was,' not 'is.'"

"Pardon?"

"She died, in 2001."

"I'm sorry. My mother died also."

A man of around Omiros's age rushes over. Cheeks flushing, he grabs and pumps Omiros's hand like a fan greeting a celebrity in an LA restaurant. He and Omiros worked together briefly last winter (*last winter!*—I can hear in their voices how it seems lifetimes ago). Omiros is cordial and courtly while talking with this Luka—who speaks good English with an Italian accent—but does not stand up or invite him to join us, though Luka keeps flicking shy glances at the empty chair at our table. Finally, Luka draws a cellphone from his parka pocket and says, "How about a picture to send to Mario and the others? Remember?" Before Omiros can reply, Luka squats down, drapes an arm over Omiros's shoulder and holds up his phone for a selfie. "No," says Omiros, turning his face away, too late.

Still crouched down, looking slightly up at Omiros, Luka says, "No pictures?"

"You have one," Omiros says softly. "This is fine. But it must not appear on Facebook or anyplace on the Net. You understand. It is for you only. You will promise me?"

"Of course!" Luka fairly shrieks, red now to the tips of his ears. "Forgive me!" He stands up and steps back from the table.

"Friend, please don't worry! But keep your promise."

After Luka withdraws, we're silent for some moments. I find I've become deeply engrossed in the cross-hatch pattern of fishbones on my plate.

"It's not always good for some people to know where you are," Omiros says.

"I understand."

"Social media is not social in the way I prefer."

I nod and raise my glass—the last of the wine—but Omiros, now reminded of phones, apps, itineraries, is looking down at his own device. "Forgive me. I must see if we are needed tonight at OXY."

I'd more or less forgotten that we have to ride back over the mountains. It's not yet 6 p.m. but fully dark beyond the windows.

Two men, a generator and a Vespa carrying twice its own weight slowly climb the hairpins cut into the cliffs above Skala. The untuned motor hacks and gargles, the headlight beam flickers. Omiros has squeezed the generator onto the footboard where his boots should rest; he's straddling the thing in place as if riding a mule.

Soon after we reach the plateau he pulls into a dirt turnaround on the inner side of the road, across from the usual crumpled guardrail and suicide drop. At the back of the turnaround, a shipping container sits rusting.

"Stavro, I want to show you something."

Seeming to feel it's important that I understand how things worked before the big NGOs arrived, when it was mainly volunteers and locals and the refugees themselves, he explains that in July this spot was an important staging area. After landing on the beach at Skala, the refugees would have to trudge up the switchback road. When they arrived here, Omiros and two other volunteers would organize and get them onto whatever buses could be found. There were far too few buses. Mostly Omiros had to send the people onward, on foot, to Mithymna and then on to Camp Moria, an eighty-five-kilometre walk south. One hot night, a thousand people slept here in the dirt of this bus lot, as he calls it. Omiros stayed awake to direct the few cars that passed that night and ensure that none accidentally crushed the sleepers.

At the end of the first week, wanting to maintain good relations with the locals, he donned rubber gloves, tied several T-shirts over his nose and mouth, went behind the empty container and, piece by piece in the heat, picked up the excrement left in the wake of several thousand people's passing through.

The word "hero" doesn't usually cue visuals of a man kneeling and filling garbage bags with human shit.

We roar on, slowly, through the mountains. To the north and far below, a dotted line of faint lights appears—the Turkish coast—as if through the window of a passenger jet. The stars brighten as the mercury dives. The side vents of my biker jacket are cinched in but the freezing wind still finds its way through.

At last Mithymna appears: a cone of lights climbing the steep hill to the spotlit castle. Quickly the town nears, growing like a constellation approached at hyper-light speed, and in fact we are now riding much faster as we roll down to the sea.

Omiros guns it with gusto up a cobblestone lane, the shuttered houses and shops reachably close on either side.

He brakes and parks the scooter against a wall, unlocks a door. I lug the generator into a messy living room/kitchen; he shares the flat with a roommate, he says. While he fills a kettle, I sit on a stool by a space heater and turn it up high. A saucer crammed with butts smoked down to the lipsticked filters sits on a coffee table beside a newsmagazine. On its cover, brown children peer through a chain-link fence, the name "Moria" sandwiched among the words—Danish, Swedish?—captioning the photo.

I wrap my icy hands around a mug of tea. Omiros sinks into the collapsed sofa and rolls another joint. After we smoke it, he pats the sofa beside him and invites me over. Does he actually like men, despite all the evidence? No, he simply means to show me a video on his smartphone—a jocular "mini-doc" slapped together for some pop-up network. Its theme is donkey fucking in Colombia, apparently an outlet for young males in rural areas. At first I force a chuckle or two, but within a few minutes I fall silent. The unlikeable host finally cuts to the money shot: an older local inserting himself into a female donkey, who seems not to notice.

"Funny, isn't it?" Omiros asks. Oddly, his stoned smile and slumped posture and enthusiasm for the video subtract little or nothing from his dignity.

"They blurred out the guy's cock," I say, "but I wish they'd blurred the faces. I mean, of the boys they interviewed."

"Yes," Omiros says instantly. "That would be better."

"I bet they would have, if they'd been American. The boys."

"Yes. If they were white… For example, in the news…" He trails off, staring past me.

"This stuff of yours is strong."

"It makes English difficult."

"White people die with their names on," I hear my voice say. "They're not part of a, an... an a..." I can't seem to palatalize "an anonymous"... nor can I organize my idea, which in this moment seems original and important: that the deeds and deaths of non-white people are expressed abstractly, statistically—this many thousands of Africans crossing from Libya into Europe, this many hundreds of Afghans killed in an ISIS attack—and not specifically, name by name, life by life... If porn is about departicular-ization, stats too can be a sort of porn.

His large, liquid pupils swivel toward me and he says earnestly, "Stavro, I can't think more about these things. Not until tomorrow, at OXY. Tonight I would rather think of... even donkeys."

"What...?"

"This funny film."

The heater hums, rattles and clicks, like a cooling engine.

"When will you go back?" he asks. "To your home."

"Soon. A few days."

"This is sad. I feel that already we are friends."

A muted knock at the door. Omiros fights his way free of the sofa, stumbles to the door, steps half-outside. I hear Klea, her raucous, grating accent: "I was hoping we could talk..." Omiros: "But it is so late now." Klea: "I think we have still some things to discuss from the summer..." They sound as if they're reading from a dialogue in an English language class, except Klea's distress is no act. Omiros steps back, she enters, it's like they're dancing, she leading, a bit

aggressively, he retreating, almost falling over the generator. She notices me. I sit up as much as the sofa and my
condition will allow.

Normally she looks pleased to see me. Not now. She
approaches and sits on the low stool in her parka and jeans,
knees together, hands tightly folded in her lap. Omiros
offers tea but, I notice, none of the hash that she must be
able to smell. Her gaze lingers on those lipstick-kissed cigarette butts as she launches into a speech about the NGOs,
how they all want to close OXY. She speaks stridently, and
when at last she looks up at Omiros and concludes—"They
want to take it away from you because you are Syrian—you
are not one of them!"—her countenance is yearning. My
presence, I guess, necessitates this code. I watch Omiros
for a signal that he wants me either to get up and leave or
to stay and referee. I want to go. I feel trapped. I feel for
Omiros, but mostly I admire Klea for her fearlessness. I try
to recall the last time I was brave enough to make myself
truly vulnerable. Whenever it was, no doubt it was around
this time of night and after a few drinks, like the ones I
smell on her.

"I am grateful for these words," Omiros says gently. "But
Stavro and I have made a midnight… deal? Yes, a deal. We
will speak only of light things tonight… things of light…"

Once I'm sure he is not trying to signal me to stay, I bid
them good night, ease the door closed and find my way to
the guest house through the silent lanes.

Street of the Silversmiths

EVERY DAY SINCE ARRIVING ON LESVOS I HAVE
walked—or, when worried I'll be late for a shift, run—
down this bone-joltingly steep, narrow lane to the lower
town and the highway. Every time, less than halfway there,
I've glanced to my right down a diverging lane that descends
between shops, houses and cafés under a trellis-like roof of
vines and branches stripped of leaves so that the sunlight
slopes through. In the warm months, foliage, flowers and
clustered grapes must shelter the lane and freckle the pavestones with shadow.

Every time I've passed that fork it has seemed more like
a portal into one of those locales your nightmind constructs:
cities where you wander and find, on turning a corner, an
unsuspected vista, vast plaza, basilica or seafront. I've told
myself every time that *next* time I won't hurry past as I

always do—always rushing and crashing past everything because I delay every departure to the last second, never budgeting a spare minute for error, exploration, unplanned encounters.

On the afternoon of December 19 I leave the guest house early, on my way to OXY for my final shift, and turn into the till-now unfollowed lane. The slope walks me downward. In Mithymna there are many streets I haven't explored but surely none as beautiful as this. The winter sun kindles a few last wisteria blooms and clumps of mummified grapes in the tree-branch trellis overhead. The shops are closed for the season, the houses for siesta. Scents of cooking seep through the lilac-coloured shutters of one house— my mother's cooking, mixed with the funeral sweetness of frankincense and myrrh, smells of boyhood Sundays.

In my mind now this signless lane is the Street of the Silversmiths—a fanciful epithet I might be remembering from some book read years ago. *A Hundred Years of Solitude*? *Midnight's Children*? A few minutes down the lane, the one-storey wall of houses on the left sheers away and over a waist-high stone wall there's a vertiginous view of the sea. How did I not realize this street must cut diagonally back along the cliffs, down to the harbour? The last building on the left is a café, open but empty, and I sit there for half an hour untouched by time.

Down on the highway I thumb a standing-room ride on a bus shuttling families from Efthalou Beach to OXY. On the thoroughly covered bosoms of the dozing women in the front rows, crucifixes rest. A teenager behind them stands up, tears off his parka and rolls his sleeve high, giving me the thumbs-up as he shows off a tattoo of an undershirted rapper brandishing a dildo-like mic. The kid, too, sports a large crucifix. "Where are you from?" I call. "Iraqi!" he calls as the friends squeezed beside him pull him back down, all of them laughing. "Iraqi, no English, Merry Christmas, sir!"

The camp is full. Packed buses like the one I've hitched in on continue to roll into the upper parking lot and let people off, while in the lower lot other buses are boarding passengers and rumbling away toward Moria. And in the heart of the camp, in front of the canteen, shrieking children are flocking and dodging around Clara Romero.

She must be at the end of her shift but shows no sign of flagging. She holds a bubble wand and a plastic water bottle full of soap. Direct in all things—her gaze, her words, her purposeful walk—she's blowing forcefully into the upturned faces of the kids who mob her and chase wobbling bubbles the size of party balloons. Kanella randomizes the game by tearing around at the edge of the scrum, lunging and snapping at any bubbles that escape the kids. I edge in and try to keep dog and children apart, though like their parents the kids are leery of dogs and swerve away when necessary. At the same time, they scream with laughter whenever the dog detonates a bubble and then urgently licks her chops, grimacing at the bitterness.

After brief negotiations Clara surrenders the bottle and wand to a small auburn-haired girl who, with an air of great pomp and significance, assumes the role of bubble-maker. Her bubbles are smaller and less mobile than Clara's but the children play on.

Beside me in cowboy boots, blue jeans and T-shirt, Clara mutters around the cigarette she's lighting. "Her name's Amina. I was lecturing her, the bubbles are for everyone. Then it occurred to me, maybe she knows that already. And whadaya know?" After a famished drag she adds in a voice even deeper than before, "That's better... At my age you want to be sure you end up dying of some worthwhile vice, not just of death."

"I get the feeling you don't confine yourself to tobacco."

"Hardly. There's also wine, Manhattans and men of a suitable ripeness. Oh, and sunshine. Look at these wrinkles."

"You look great," I say. "Kanella! Come here, *ela' dho*!"

"You may be ripening, but you've got work to do. Ten years and you'll be a better liar."

"I'm pretty good already, especially to myself."

"Oh, but you get *worse* at those ones—the lies you tell yourself. That's part of the ripening."

A bubble floats past, iridescing like a gasoline puddle. She sends a smoke ring after it and says, "Such lovely weather for the camp's last stand, no?"

"What, already? But I thought... maybe not until spring."

"December thirty-first, Omiros thinks now. Which makes sense for Big NGO scheduling, Q4 reports, etcetera etcetera." She chuckles hoarsely. "Efficiency in all the ways that don't matter."

"He's here, right? He said he would be today. I need to say goodbye."

"He'll be here every day until the end."

Clara and I join Asim, Jaquon and Cyrus in the boarding zone and within minutes the bubble-game players and their families are striding down the prayer-flagged lanes toward the coaches. A pale, very tall man in an IRC bib deems himself to be supervising the process. This is a smaller team of helpers than usual, since over a dozen volunteers have just departed for Christmas. Luckily the camp's systems have been refined enough that a skeleton crew can manage.

Today's playlist eddies between jaunty Greek pop and Bob Marley's Greatest Hits. The reggae songs that leap out here are "Exodus," a Greek name for a Jewish refugee journey of some 3,400 years ago, and "Redemption Song," where the human traffickers are pirates, and the profiteers are the skippers of merchant ships—players in the slave trade that globalized capitalism and whose psychopathy still operates in its subconscious.

The red-haired Amina, enthroned on her papa's shoulders with her bubble sceptre, haughtily looks down as I collect his infinity-sign chit. She's achieving plumper bubbles now and they float dreamily over the marching lines of people. Again the hopefulness of forward motion is tangible and catching, though for the volunteers it's muted by uncertainty, a sense that things are rapidly changing and closing down. OXY, of course, is closing, but more importantly the borders of Europe are being sealed. Do these people know it? According to Asim, the Arabic-speakers try to keep up with the news but tend to regard unfavourable reports as mere rumour, like hungry folks who have waited hours in a queue and, pushing forward, refuse to believe the soup wicket ahead really has closed and locked. Refugees don't just flee from, they flee to, and none would choose to end up here in a broken, jobless country that can't accommodate them and where their presence would be a further burden on their hosts.

By sunset we've run out of buses. The remaining eighty-four refugees, Syrian, Iranian, Yemeni, will stay overnight. I'm walking toward the canteen to see if help is needed there when Clara hails me from just inside the first tent shelter. She's seated at the arm wrestling table beside the scarecrow Christmas tree, taking on all comers—a group of nine or ten boys and girls. She's knackered now, she says, and needs a smoke and something to eat back at the Elektra. Would I take over here? She stands up and we hug goodbye, since I'll be leaving first thing in the morning and probably won't see her again. Through her coat, she seems all rib cage and spine. "Whatever you do," she orders me, "don't just *let* them win! No one else is going to, from here on!"

I nod. "Oh, have you seen Omiros anywhere?"

"I hear he had to go to Anastasia House, then meet some NGO types in town. I'm sure he'll be back before too late."

For a while I arm-wrestle many-armed teams of children. Then some young men approach, addressing me in a language I assume is Farsi, and I invite them to take over. In the canteen I help Larry and Iphigenia serve lentil stew and distribute juice packs while Kanella sleeps on a blanket under one of the tables. Puppies due fairly soon in the New Year, obviously. The NGO reps keep insisting that we evict her from the canteen, and we have, half-heartedly, but she simply slips back in when the door is being opened or closed. No one knows what will become of her when OXY shuts down, though a few volunteers are talking adoption.

By 7 p.m. everyone has eaten and is settling in for the night. Under a floodlight on the patch of ground where the Green Helmets work, I find scraps of wood, raid the tool boxes and set about building shelving for the women's clothing tent. In the men's tent, Dieter and Oskar are reorganizing, arguing in German, while a stone's throw farther north three men take down the army-green platoon tents the volunteers have never actually used. They're debating the procedure in Greek—probably townspeople hired for a few hours.

An hour later, the tents are down and I'm still trying to get my shelves to stand. While two of the Greeks tie their load into the bed of a truck, the third strolls over and says, "Friend, let me help."

His name is Iosip and he knows carpentry. While gently mocking my slaphammer joins and ill-measured cuts, he helps clean up and finish the job. If he sees the creation of furniture for a facility in the process of being dismantled as quixotic, he keeps the opinion to himself. We carry the shelving unit into the women's tent, situate it and fill it with cardboard boxes that have been sitting on the damp ground. When I urge him to get in touch if he ever travels to North America, he says, "Ah, we Greeks are poor now and can only dream."

The overnight shift starts to arrive, another skeleton crew. Pericles vaults off his scooter and detains my hand in both of his; I brace for a sweep or a tackle. But this really is just a handshake. I ask him if he knows whether Omiros will arrive soon. He thinks maybe Omiros rode down to Mytilene to pick up Lindsay, already returning from her stress leave in England.

"Let's hit the road, Steve," Larry calls, sounding weary.

"One moment!" says Pericles, feinting and then contorting me into a chokehold. While I squirm, he says loudly, "Stavro, I have news! I have found a good job in Canada. Next month I go."

"Great," I say, my voice stifled by his armpit. "Where is it?"

"A strange name. A cowboys-and-Indians name. In Greek, *Aspro-alogo*."

"Whitehorse… Take a bigger parka."

"Pardon?"

"Cold there!"

"The colder place is where there is no job, Stavro. Come, I'll show you a trick to escape this one."

Larry gives Iphigenia and me a ride back to town in his wheezing Westphalia camper. Chet Baker, displeased that I've usurped the hair-covered front seat, broods at me with wet, saggy eyes, his muzzle resting by the shift. The night is moonless, the camper's headlamps the only light between OXY and the town. We round a cliffside bend and a lone headlight flies at us and flashes past: I see a large man comically upright on a small machine, his trenchcoat fanning behind him like a spoiler.

"I believe that was the boss," Larry says.

"We'll say goodbye for you, Stavro," says Iphigenia, leaning forward between the front seats, stroking Chet Baker's ears, baby-talking to him in Greek.

This is what people do

THE MORNING BREAKS CLEAR AND STILL AND THE AIR
has a ravishing freshness as I head down toward the highway, a duffle bag and satchel over my shoulders. I stop at the
bakery and then at the ingeniously crammed little grocery
shop, its aisles narrow in proportion to the narrowness of
the town's lanes.

As I wait for change at the checkout counter by the
open door, an old woman, across the lane in her own doorway, calls to me. I can't understand. She is nodding and
beckoning. The tall, freckled woman behind the counter
shows a genial gap between her front teeth and says, "Your
husband needs a help."

"Her husband needs help?"

"Her husband, yes. You leave your bread and juices here."

I step across the lane and follow the woman inside, ducking under a medievally low lintel. The house is damp, cool and scented with an aromatic spice I recall suddenly from childhood, when it would lend its strange bittersweetness to *tsoureki*, the braided Easter loaf. What was its name? The black-layered widows at the gatherings we attended after holiday communions always smelled of it.

This woman, like the widows, is short and stout and has blue-rinsed, tied-back hair, though her housedress is not black but yellow with a faded red poppy motif. Briskly she leads me down a hallway as low and dark as a gallery in a mine. Ahead, a naked, seemingly loinclothed figure is slumped in a door frame, a toilet and bathtub behind him. He looks ancient enough to be her century-old father and at the same time infantile, a great-grandchild, the skin of his hairless head and body albino white. Head bulbous, limbs eaten away so the joints look huge and swollen. As we approach, his face lolls toward us, the pale eyes pleading. His forearm and hand lie on the tiled floor twitching as if trying to rise. His lips quiver; there's a faint whimpering studded with other sounds, maybe attempts at words. I go to him while the woman, now behind me, instructs me in Greek, rapidly but calmly, almost casually, as if this is a routine predicament. *Fallen… can't lift him… please help.*

A stubble-faced foreigner in heavy boots and a black leather jacket looms over him as he peers up with a child's scared eyes. He lifts both his wizened arms to me. *Pick me up.* The loincloth is a geriatric diaper. He's wedged in place, the back of his head and shoulders against one side of the door frame, his knees raised, bare toes curled against the other side. There's a smell, either from the toilet or from

him. I grip his upraised arms by the wrists and pull. Useless.
The woman keeps instructing me in words I don't get—I'm
not even listening—then I realize I have to slip in behind
him somehow and lift from under his arms. Because he's so
limp, I'm able to squeeze my legs in behind his back, bend
down, work my forearms under his armpits and hoist. He
slowly comes upright. I can feel him helping with what
little strength he has. His wife too is reaching in, gripping
his elbow.

I keep my arms hammer-gripped high under his armpits—a puppeteer with a life-sized figure—and shuffle him
up another dim mineshaft, he silent, the woman amiably
directing me. "*Etsi, etsi, endaksi!*" I walk bow-legged, boots
splayed out, anxious not to trample his bed-sored heels. He
smells faintly of diaper and something else, a mortuary
smell, a deodorizer of some kind? We pass through a sitting
room with a shuttered window—the only window I've seen
in here. The room is a gallery of ikons and framed photographs, many black and white, some sepia: rows of faces,
couples, children, uniformed men... generations glimpsed
and falling away like painted faces in a Byzantine tomb lit
for a moment in passing.

"*Stripste aristera,*" she says—*turn left*. A short hallway,
then a windowless lamplit room mostly filled by a double bed. Its coverlet is neatly turned down. A dark towel
laid over one side. I shuffle him toward that side. Over
his withered haunches the diaper has been loosening and
now the right tab pulls free. The diaper droops. As I look
down—fearing it will fall off, now seeing the extensive shit-
smear inside—the woman's hand casually darts in, a couple
of inches from my crotch, and makes a quick adjustment,

"*Etsi, endaksi!*", as unfazed as if she has just straightened the knot of his necktie at church.

I sit him on the edge of the bed and step back and he looks up at me and wheezes something, maybe thank you. The woman, still clucking cheerfully, holds out a spritzer bottle containing a liquid the colour of antifreeze. "*Ta heria sou,*" she says: *your hands*. I glance at the old man. Will this measure further humiliate him? But he's staring absently at the wall. I show my palms, the woman sprays them, the room fills with the censer perfumes of Orthodox Eucharist and some other unguent, too, maybe sandalwood. I nod to the old man and we leave him sitting on the bed. The woman guides me back out via that same convoluted route; the house is not large but its walls and spaces fold in on themselves.

At the front door she thanks me in her no-nonsense way. Nothing in her posture suggests a readiness to accept a parting hug, and now it hits me: the embrace of two healthy beings out here in the sunshine would exclude him, isolate him further, while serving to consecrate the relief of a man who can simply walk away, virtue enhanced, from this crisis too.

"He is ninety-five!" she announces with pride.

She bustles off, leaving the door ajar. I cross the street in that virginal air and inebriating light, a bit stunned. I've just been a mile underground. The woman in the shop displays that friendly gap in her grin as she hands me some coins. No remark or question about my detour, as if it happens to customers all the time.

Loaded with luggage and supplies I jolt down the cobblestone lane toward the bus stop, checking my watch.

Greek public transit debunks all those smug neo-liberal
axioms about Southern tardiness and inefficiency. As usual,
I've left no wiggle room. I'm not going to make it. I pause
and set my bags down on a bench at the corner where the
Street of the Silversmiths forks away toward the harbour
and the Captain's Kitchen.

The trellised wisteria are even sparser now.

A few seconds of vertigo, a sudden upward convulsion
unstoppable as orgasm and I'm sobbing, choking and shaking, pulling my hat brim over my lowered face, one arm
out, hand braced against the wall, helpless—my body a
passive channel through which some great grief is surging,
surfacing with unearthly sounds, dying animal sounds. I
grind my face into the wall trying to stem them... Her
ease and directness and trust, how she thought nothing of
summoning a stranger to assist with her soiled and dying
husband, no apologies for inconveniencing me, no polite,
perfunctory questions about me or my presence in Greece,
no embarrassment about her husband's disintegration. *He
is my man in any case; and you will help me because this is
what people do.*

As the gasping sobs subside, a word brims up, as if from
the same churning source, *mahlepi*, that Easter spice I first
smelled half a century ago in my mother's kitchen.

I stand at the bus stop at the edge of town in a post-
cathartic trance and something else returns, the old
Japanese marriage proposal, *Won't you share my tomb with
me?* It seemed ghoulish when I first heard of it, at twenty-
five, in Japan. But back then I was afraid of death itself.
Now what seems worse is the likelihood of dying in a place
that ostracizes death and quarantines those embarked on

the crossing; a place that would rather not know, not reach out across the cold.

My bus is vanishing around a cliffside turn above the sea.

On the hull of her coffin, my father, against all expectation, collapsed and sobbed *Wait for me, wait for me, wait for me.*

I've no home to return to, I see, just a place I can no longer belong in.

Afghan Hill

A DODDERING LADA PULLS UP IN FRONT OF THE STOP.
The driver—a volunteer I've seen several times but never
met—has a face of cowboy crags and clefts and a pompa-
dour of receding blond hair under a baseball cap pushed
back so the brim grazes the roof. Auburn mutton chops,
drooping cigarette.

"Austin T. Rosenkrantz III," he says. "I'm heading down
to Mordor for the afternoon shift. Hear they're short."

"Steve. That's what I hear too and that's where I'm going."

"Smoke?"

"No, thanks."

He tosses his barely begun cigarette out the window.
"Let's see if this old vestige can get us there, huh? Borrowed
it from Klea."

A few minutes later we pass OXY. Austin, eyes forward, fixed on the cliffside road, fist-bumps the horn and lifts his arm out the window in a lazy wave. People I don't recognize are dismantling the men's clothing tent. Cyrus and Klea, stooped like gleaners, are collecting garbage while Delilah chins herself off the eaves of the canteen hut. An Arabic pop song is blasting. No sign of Omiros, but isn't that Lindsay (flash of lavender-streaked hair) crouched under the canteen wicket, patting Kanella?

Austin lacks the twang to suit his burnsides, cap and good old boy aspect. In a dude-ish California upspeak he rambles engagingly, a miscellany of leftist opinion, stoned-seeming neo-hippie affect and oldfangled American masculinism. He is a gun owner. He is a gun user. Like his old man before him, he served in the US Navy, and during the First Gulf War he received medals he was once very proud of. But like other thoughtful veterans—Paul Fussell, Hugh Thompson, U.S. Grant—he came to see clearly what he only glimpsed at the time, through tiny rifts in a grinding daily rota expressly conceived to pre-empt reflection: each *casus belli* is a cynical lie. But how many twenty-year-olds really grasp historical and political contexts, and where would recruiting drives be if they did? After the war, he embarked on a solo project of comprehensive historical reading and now, in his mid-forties, is appalled by Western military adventures in the Middle East, "going back to World War I," as he puts it, though I argue that they go much farther back, and he agrees, the nineteenth century, the eighteenth, the Crusades.

A few minutes down the highway, we pass a slight figure walking on the narrow shoulder of the road, trustingly, his back to the traffic. Sandals, white yoga pants, orange parka, wool cap. He carries nothing. I turn and glance out the back window. So Klaus has resumed his Peace Walk. He has said he will head next to the Holy Land, then across the Sinai into Egypt and south through Africa. For today he follows the refugees' route, an eight-hour walk down to Moria and Mytilene.

The outlines of the mountains against the sky are razor clean. Our road now skirts the sea. Through the windows come the infant cries of the shearwaters. Is Austin here to atone for his participation in a stage of the refugee-making process? But that's his subtext, his shadow, and I say nothing.

He guides me up the stony face of Afghan Hill through a dense *favela* of pup tents and tarpaulin lean-tos. Allegorically thin figures hunker around fires fuelled by rubbish and plastic bottles that give feeble green flames, sooty fumes and a sweetly noxious stink. The clothes hung out to dry anywhere a line can be strung seem to have been washed in mud. Everywhere are stumps and skeletons of olive trees, branches snapped, the bark peeled.

One such amputee marks the hill's crest.

On the far side lies the camp's registration hub: a former military compound enclosed by a high chain-link fence topped with concertina wire. Inside this Stalag, dozens of white UNHCR huts have been crammed. Here Syrian and other families are meant to be sheltered before they proceed to nearby Mytilene and the ferry to Athens—but now in their numbers they spill out beyond the fence and over the hill, a tapering queue of maybe a thousand new arrivals, all waiting to be registered.

On the dirt road that bisects the camp, near the crest of the hill, we pass a row of catering trucks—cheap shoes, blankets, fast food—and two vending machines offering soft drinks and coffee. The machines look shockingly clean and new amid all the grime, garbage and sprawling disorder. There are lineups of people in soiled denim or drab layers, browns, blacks, greys—only a few parkas and some of the women's headscarves sampling the brighter part of the spectrum that must still exist beyond this place. More lineups at the clothing tents, tea tent, food tent. We pass journalists in sport-adventure gear, posed in front of cameras, soberly speaking into mics while curious young refugees cluster behind them; we pass a few NGO reps, idle as pylons, of course, though their usual expressions of officious territoriality have faded into stares of helpless stupefaction.

At the fenceless edge of the camp, where the dirt road ends, we stop. The stony expanse ahead and to either side bristles with mutilated trees and is land-mined with excrement. (Long queues outside the few porta-toilets: obviously folks sneak up here before dawn or after dark.)

Austin issues me a cigarette and lights his and mine against the stench, two gravediggers on a battlefield.

"This place is just hell," I say.

"To some of them it's home. Some have been stuck here for months. Place was set up for hundreds, not thousands— most densely populated place in the world now, I hear." He spits and checks his watch. "All right, *compañero*, we're on."

* * *

He's working security detail outside the women's clothing-change tent. Journalists have been trying to slip in and sneak photos of refugee women unscarved, or unwhat-evered. "Didn't have to bounce anybody last week," he says, cowboy laconic, "but beware the wrath of a peaceful man." I offer to help but he wants to introduce me to the folks at the men's dry-clothing depot, they're always short a few hands.

Instantly assigned to crowd control, I relieve a moon-faced youth with side-parted hair and acne blooming across his brow. Short-sleeved dress shirt, dark slacks—he looks like a Peace Corps volunteer *circa* 1960. In a Midwestern accent he blurts, "Thank you, sir. Thank God. I hope it goes all right for you. We've been on since five a.m."

I'm meant to manage a bottleneck in front of the cloth-ing depot, letting refugees through one at a time so the volunteers behind me can properly serve them. The tight-packed queue recedes and curves out of sight behind a large military tent, the men's change room. Like a human turnstile I stand between wooden stakes and hold the noosed end of a length of pink rope—maybe cut from a skipping rope?—that's knotted to one of the stakes. I hold the rope clear—"*Marhabaan*, welcome"—and a soaked man enters and goes to the service slot. I loop the noose over the other stake. It seems simple and proves so for the first five minutes, but the queue, pressured from behind and unable or unwilling to resist, keeps swelling forward, the men in front stretching the rope until I have to stand before it, raising my hands, pleading with them to retreat. And they do—they smile, they nod, they back up, they urge their shivering comrades to back up. But a few seconds later they resume pushing, unconsciously and inexorably as a glacier.

On the other side of a row of crowd-control fences, the women's queue has packed into a dense column jamming forward, shrieking mothers and grandmothers elbowing to the front, holding or dragging children. In a gap between two wooden stakes a sunburned Englishman with a professorial accent is shouting like King Canute confronting the tide. "Ladies, please—one by one! Step back, ladies, *please*!" They will not. He is having to let through several at a time.

Now it's happening here too. Whenever I lift the rope—"*Marhabaan... wahid, wahid!*"—two, three, even four men squeeze through, some ignoring me while others put hands to their hearts and, grinning sadly, say words that might mean *These are my two brothers... This is my family... We four are friends... We have walked together from Aleppo.*

Behind me Diomedes, a local with a kindly face and uncommonly good English, is struggling: six men crowd his wicket and talk over each other while he raises his hands and repeats, "One by one, please!" It's my fault. I would rather address the refugees or otherwise make contact—eye contact, a handshake—than maintain order. But order is what's needed now. Over the heads of the six men Diomedes peers desperately. "Stavro, please, do your job!" As I wave to assure him I will, a teenager caped in a thermal blanket ducks under the rope. I try standing in the gap again. A packed column of bodies, faces expressionless, inch toward and into me. The crowd has merged into a single creature.

A young guy with a good haircut but distressed clothing and duct-taped shoes says, "You have cigarette, thank you?" I hand him the extra that Austin gave me and let him past.

Now an older man with a pitted face and small, angry eyes puts out his hand—"Cigarette!"—and when I shrug and apologize he snarls some thick, guttural phrase. The men around him look aghast, then hush and scold him.

To my left the Englishman has been brushed aside and stands dabbing his scalp with a handkerchief like a white flag.

At some point—I've lost track of time—a grating Yankee voice starts barking to my left, "Back up, back up now!" I glance over. A small woman with a ponytail sprouting from the vent in the back of her baseball cap is restoring order. She sounds like a coxswain or a hockey coach. Minutes later she appears beside me: cold colourless eyes, braces on her teeth. "Hi, I'm Wendy. I've been doing this for a couple weeks. You need to get control here." She steps into the gap, lifts her little hands and hollers at the men as she did at the women. They retreat. "See? Just make yourself clear!" She's right. My feel-good approach worked perfectly well at OXY, with its smaller, calmer crowds, but clearly Moria makes different demands. Would I have lasted a month here?

After I leave the queue to her, a man in a Translators Without Borders jacket asks me to mind an old woman slumped on the seat of her walking frame: "She awaits her son to return in dry clothes. She is afraid of that animal"—he points at a black mastiff guarding a warehouse beyond a safety fence a long stone's throw away—"and she does not want to be alone. I have told her you speak no Kurdish—it's no problem."

He hurries off and the woman begins talking—at first, I assume, about the pacing dog, which she points toward, but then about other things, surely, since she continues in her gentle, froggy voice for over twenty minutes, increasingly animated, as if she believes I'm beginning to catch on, though without ever meeting my gaze, looking away whenever I try to catch her eye, looking anywhere but at me. Her sagging lids all but hide her eyes, a faded hazel colour.

I'm to find Austin before sunset so we can drive down to Mytilene. While looking for him, I stumble on the Kinder Kingdom. ABSOLUTELY NO PICTURES OR VIDEOS WITH OUT PERMISSION!!, reads a handwritten sign stuck to the side of the family-sized tent. I peer in through the blurry plastic window: children kneeling at tables improvised from fruit crates and busily scribbling with pencil crayons or painting with watercolours. A young woman volunteer sits with them. Outside the tent, a few girls and boys are shooting baskets—deflated soccer ball and small, warped hoop the height of my chest—while two girls sit on plastic chairs at a plastic table with a toy teapot, pretending to sip from thimble cups. The PVC palm tree overhanging the table accents the impression of a small, artificial oasis.

A skinny man in a Kraftwerk T-shirt flutters out and demands, "You are a journalist?"

"No, a volunteer," I say, "need any help here? This place is beautiful!"

I back up as he squints, jittery, one red eye twitching; then his brow unclenches, though his hands stay fisted at his hips.

"Help not required but I thank you. I have worked hard to create this refuge here—but you see this sign that I must make? Journalists! The children's privacy must be protected, *ja*, and their innocence, even here the innocence. Especially here! Some journalists have intruded to take pictures."

"Maybe the same ones Austin is planning to assault," I say. "Are you sure—"

"Austin, *ja*, I like this man. But these journalists I can assault myself."

The soccer ball skitters off toward a huddle of volunteers and I race one of the boys to it, trapping it under my sole and rolling it back to him. My little sprint has brought me to the huddle. A young Scotsman with a dashing ridge of black hair, heroic stubble and a leather coat with sheepskin trim is briefing the others: on the far side of Afghan Hill, a riot squad is preparing to push back the Syrians who have been waiting all day to register. The situation is serious.

Follow me.

I have to run a few steps every dozen or so to keep up with him and the others—Moria volunteers are adept at dodging throngs like the ones now flowing downhill against us. I keep losing sight of our leader, his white sheepskin collar. The sun is setting behind the stripped, pillaged trees and the enormous tent city.

We regroup outside the high-fenced compound. Inside, back of the chain-link gates, officials stand scowling and smoking at the registration tables. Why are no refugees being allowed in to register? A dozen riot cops with transparent shields stand looking out through the fence at the pressing crowd. Crowd, not queue; the pressure of a thousand distressed people edging forward has created a dense swelling at the front, where folks are not so much pushing as being pushed against the locked gates. Maybe five hundred are packed into a mass there, while a tapering comet tail of others recedes far behind, disappearing over the hill.

The young Scotsman explains that the cops are refusing to admit anyone until the crowd forms two lines—one for families, one for single men—because they want to register families first and settle them inside the compound, for safety's sake, overnight. But there are no Arabic translators today, so the head cop has been bullhorning the orders in English and Greek. Now he wants the volunteers to try to convey them. "We've got to move these people back into two lines or the goon squad means to charge. They give us twenty minutes." He offers several Arabic phrases to use, though his tentative delivery suggests he's repeating them phonetically, maybe incorrectly.

As the floodlights brighten above the gate, dusk falling fast, the chief starts broadcasting with the megaphone again. We split up and hurry along the edges of the crowd, urging people to move back and separate into two lines by pointing and using the phrase *Wahid eayila*—supposedly Arabic for *one family*. A face from Efthalou Beach looms into focus: the John C. Reilly avatar. He recognizes me and smiles warmly, we shake hands, I stride on up the narrowing queue miming and reciting that phrase, probably deforming it further each time.

A dignified little man with a white goatee, maybe a retired schoolteacher, asks how much longer they will have to wait. "We stand eight hour and no toilet—the toilets are inside the fence!"

"Please move back," I say and ask him to tell the others about the lines. "Wait—can you come to the front with me to translate?"

"If I move back or front, I lose my place, maybe wait all night!"

I shake my head *no*, yet it could be true. "Please."

"I must stay in line!"

"Then tell the others here, OK? Two lines!"

"Why you treat us like we are not people?"

"I'm sorry," I mutter, unable to meet his eyes as I move on.

That amplified, reverbing voice keeps hectoring the Syrians in Greek and English, and now some of them begin yelling back and in moments the yelling starts to cohere into a pounding chant. I and a couple of other volunteers are working maybe a hundred metres from the gates, back where the queue actually is a queue and the people seem less desperate, as if they only just arrived. They're politely retreating and forming a single file, though this minor adjustment seems unlikely to relieve the crush at the front.

"Thank God," says a volunteer behind me. I glance toward the gates. They're swinging inward, surely to admit refugees? Yet the echoing voice keeps ordering, "BACK, BACK, MOVE BACK NOW!" An awful shudder runs through the crowd. The Arabic chant intensifies, then there's another, faster beat, a contra-rhythm, maybe the cops smashing their truncheons on their shields. What I can see is the white tops of their helmets glinting in the floodlight, pushing out through the gates in a single rank.

I run toward the front, glimpse the police chief standing to one side, gaping, the megaphone hanging from his hand. I start toward him. A woman steps out of the crowd and blocks me. "*Monsieur, parlez-vous français?*" She doesn't wait for an answer but starts explaining in loud yet leisurely French (*speak faster!* I want to beg her) that she's searching for her husband and son. She's very pregnant. A pert, girlish face.

Arcs of light draw my gaze up over her head—truncheons scything the air above the crowd and flailing down, hands shooting up. The chant dissolves into screams as the mob dissolves, exploding in all directions, hundreds of people with blank, blind eyes. The woman and I are in their path. Facing me, she can't see them coming—she's on a shore with her back turned to a tsunami—but she sees my eyes, looks behind. I grab her elbow: "Go, go, go!" Together we're running, the furious slapping of hundreds of shoes closing in. She rips free of me and, somehow unindered by her belly and long tunic, pulls ahead. I realize I'm slowing down on purpose—men bolting past on either side—my instinct now to walk with planted steps, extend my arms, brace for impact.

My god this is happening.

The ones overtaking me are slowing too, the mob momentum and panic subsiding as fast as it erupted. I stop and pivot. Many who were fleeing just a moment ago have reversed and seem equally frantic to reclaim positions near the front, even if it means facing the cops again. No sign of the woman. From somewhere the shrilling of a whistle blown over and over. I run back toward the front of the crowd. Who knows what I'm thinking—what I hope I can possibly achieve.

With other volunteers I stand perpendicular to the battle-front between the cops and the Syrians—all men, many of them young. Again that shattering, needle-sharp whistle, blast after blast. Somewhere the chief is babbling a stream of Greek words through the megaphone. The cops in their Cylon body armour pound their clubs against their shields, or use the shields to bump back refugees while threatening with the clubs. The features of the stout little cop nearest me, a few steps away, clench and contort, teeth gritted under his dapper moustache as he tries in his terror to terrify this mob—also terrified—into backing off. In garbled English he brays, "*Ko pack, ko pack, ko pack*" and bulges his eyes—it's a rugby haka with far higher stakes. My throat swells closed for a second, then I and a few others are calling, "Stop it, stop this!" and in Greek, "*Siga, siga!*" The cops hear nothing, their peripheral hearing and vision voided. Battle-brain. A small volunteer dressed like a goth is sobbing and I put my arm around her shoulder.

The front-line Syrians cry out and gesticulate, eyes petitioning, eyes indignant. They must want to retreat before these armoured men, like the armed men they fled in Syria, yet they must want to hold their ground and not lose their place, not lose any more time. Their wills lean in only one direction, forward, through lineups and across borders, even as the borders ahead start to close; to be forced backward here, even fifty steps, is agony—yet to fight the local authorities might be fatal to the dream, so now they do start to withdraw, ten steps, twenty, until the impulse spreads through the crowd and they're all retreating steadily.

We walk back along the queue, mainly single men now, urging them to keep moving back, *Arjouk, arjouk, shukhran*! Beyond the queue, under the fence beside the gates, another group is congregating—families, most of them already seated, either in submission or in exhausted relief. Those maddening whistle blasts start up again and now I see: a small boy wandering on the periphery of the seated group,

tooting a whistle. But the megaphone is silent. The cops
are silent. A collective response has kicked in, the mass of
us, refugees, volunteers, cops, instinctively collaborating to
de-escalate and pacify.

A man wearing a space blanket like a poncho, having
cut a hole for his head, grips my hand. While he is frail,
the identical twin behind him, leaning on a steel cane, is
cadaverous. "Friend, you look!" says the man, kneeling and
lifting the hems of his brother's black jeans above geriatric
shoes with Velcro tabs.

Instead of shins, thin metal pegs.

"Ten hours he waits! Where is there water?"

I lead them to the front of the queue and approach the
police chief, his cap pushed back off his streaming brow.
The skin around his eyes has that bruised Levantine look,
though the eyes are not the usual brown but a pale, liquid
green. Despite his glower and the uniform he looks vulnerable, a grieving son at the end of a funeral. Beautiful,
lugubrious eyes. I gesture toward the man with the cane and
speak in fractured Greek. The chief cuts me off in English:
"It does not matter where he stands. We will not begin this
line for three more hours." An armoured cop behind him
adds something in Greek and a second later I get it: *Or
six more hours*. Still, I take the man and his brother to the
front, where the others nod, make room and welcome him
in subdued voices. I haven't the heart—to say nothing of
the words—to explain about the long wait in store.

I wander back through the dark, seething camp to find my
ride. A figure emerges from under a stripped tree and asks

for a cigarette. His face is in deep shadow, as if redacted. I dig out the Greek tobacco and papers I rarely use and struggle to roll him one, my nerves still on vibrato. Another faceless man materializes. "Cigarette?" I start to roll a second one, fumble, drop the packet, pick it up, remember Austin must be looking for me. More men are converging on us: "Friend, you from America?" Suddenly feeling helpless to help, I push the tobacco, papers and lighter on the first man—"Here, please!"—and flee. I believe that's exactly the right word. I have spent some six hours—not even a full shift—in Moria and am half-giddy with relief at the prospect of escape.

I want to hide the truth

THE NEXT DAY IN MYTILENE I HAVE A FEW HOURS before boarding the ferry for Athens, so I check my duffle bag and walk south along the coast, away from the city. Rafts have been arriving daily on this desolate stretch of sand and pebble beach; maybe I can help out for a few hours. But while I pass dozens of beached rafts, and dunes of orange life vests, I don't see a soul. Hardly a car or truck on the beachside highway. At noon, the sun still low, I turn back. A dump truck shudders past, its bed heaped with deflated rafts and countless life vests that mysteriously stay put, not flying off the back in the wind.

In a waterfront café I wait to board the night ferry. Beside me, a well-to-do Syrian family, presumably also waiting, sits eating a meal, which for the five children seems to involve rounds of french fries. A bearded, paunchy patriarch and two headscarved women. The children seem sullen, the adults cheerful and friendly.

An hour after dark I board with hundreds of refugees, some of whom stake out the clean-looking floor space under the stairways to the upper decks. Others—not many—line up in front of the hotel-style reception desk and receive keys for the overnight cabins.

On the congested stairway as I climb to the upper deck to get a parting view of Lesvos, my eye zooms in on one of the descending faces. I almost stumble. Tender, almost tearful pale-green eyes, the skin around them discoloured as if contused... it's the police chief from Moria, though now he sports a snappy Tahitian shirt and ironed khakis. Is he on leave and travelling to Athens, or is he on plainclothes detail, keeping an eye on some of the young Syrian men he must have registered late last night or early this morning? The mounting and descending crowds bear us past each other, inches apart; his face recoils as he meets my stare and tries to place me.

I have a sandwich and an ouzo in the bar. On my way out, I pass two refugees conferring in front of a map that covers a large wall: the Greek mainland, the Aegean Sea, the islands and the Turkish coast. I join them but before I can point to our position, the elder—an ex-boxer or -wrestler, cauliflower ear and crooked nose—says, "It is surprise. The guide in Turkey tells us, you will land near Athens. But only now we go to Athens?" He taps his middle finger on the dotted line marking the ferry's route. "Are we now here?"

"I think so. Right around there."

"We are brothers, from Afghanistan. Our families are at rest"—he looks and gestures upward, as if he might mean heaven. "We find space on the top, outside. We were walking for five weeks."

His younger brother examines the map, his face inches from the wall.

"Did you actually have a 'guide,'" I ask, "or do you mean…" I'm about to say *smuggler*, *trafficker*, but now wonder if the terms might seem insulting—as if he and his family are closer to contraband than people. But now he tells me, "I mean the human smuggler. Many of them on the journey. They were not all cruel, but none were friends. But now we are here and happy." As he says the word *happy* his face hardly looks it, but then it's apparent how hard he is concentrating on finding the English words.

In the early morning darkness and cold I disembark with the other foot passengers, mostly refugees. They gather in their various groups, waiting for the buses that will take them into Athens, while I indulge one of the signal privileges of any volunteer: being able to walk away at will and at leisure. I follow signs to the metro and board an empty train. Some twenty stops later, I sleepwalk onto a deserted platform with my duffle bag, forgetting my satchel, which contains the Greek primer my mother used almost seventy years ago, her neat schoolgirl handwriting squeezed into the margins, and the Lesvos journal in which I've filled eighty pages with notes. I pivot, yell uselessly and watch, through the door of the ghost train, as the satchel glides away, resting on its own seat in a car headed north for the end of the line. I feel both queasily weak and pumped up, as if a medic has just spiked me with adrenalin.

Alone in the echoing station I tell myself certain things and call myself certain names. Is there any line finer than the one between feeling positive, or at least OK, and like an irredeemable fuck-up?

My Greek grandmother once said something to the effect that I could trust her but not other Greeks—they were *klepsei-klepsei*, as she put it, rubbing her thumb against her middle and index fingers, a shrewd glitter in her eye. I figure my satchel is long gone. So does the lone metro employee I manage to find upstairs in the station. But as it happens, some thoughtful soul will soon turn it in, and by 9 a.m. I will be setting out from a chain hotel near the Acropolis to retrieve it from the police station before embarking on a last little volunteer journey.

I'm planning to visit Athens's main transit camp, said to be located in a disused 2004 Olympics site, a tae kwon do stadium on the southern edge of the city. With just thirty hours left until my flight, I've decided not to contact my few distant relations here, having learned during a visit some years ago that seeing Greek kin means relinquishing all personal plans and freedom—such is the hospitality, generosity and energy of one's hosts. Decision made, I feel lightened and yet faintly rueful. These relatives are among my last blood links to my mother and grandmother. I am making strangers my priority.

Of course, that's what I came here to do.

The streets I follow to the police station are surprisingly lively, given the view from my hotel window before dawn.

When I'd entered the room, the curtains were open and the high window looked out on a metropolis as dark as any blacked-out wartime city. The houses and apartment blocks seemed abandoned, as if the residents had all fled for ancestral villages. A few storeys down, beyond an alley where rubbish was smouldering, a single window showed light: the bald head of a man sitting on a couch viewing an action movie on a large screen.

After happily retrieving my satchel, journal, and that precious textbook, I walk on with a snap in my step. Relief has left me temporarily immune to the local misery, which in fact I could avoid altogether if I stuck to the larger streets and the tourist zone, where wealthy Greeks and foreigners, mainly group-tour Chinese, are taking the morning sun on restaurant patios. But dogleg down side streets and the shops are derelict, the high walls a palimpsest of spray paint graffiti. Just blocks from the Acropolis, in an alley reeking of ammonia, two junkies, rigid as mimes, sit across from each other shooting up.

I shortcut through a sprawling meat market like a wax museum of animal atrocities, heads intact, faces staring, the bloated, burgundy livers left in the cavities of the pendant bodies. Little flensed creatures slung by their feet seem to be lambs until I notice their small cotton tails and white fur socks.

Looking for the metro I pass several families bivouacked in the street. I recognize a family now, the parents' haggard young faces vaguely familiar, the child's vividly so: a rosebud nose bubbling snot, cavernous black eyes gazing up. I am a make-believe border guard on a pier after dark, welcoming her to a safer shore. The father looks past me while the headscarved mother, eyes on the sidewalk, holds out her hand. I dig out a bill while the girl stares. Her cheeks are still plump, her parents' faces aged and thinner.

As I walk on I hear the woman muttering, maybe to the next passerby, *Give me job, I am something useless.*

In Exarchia, the anarchist enclave, Antifa flags hang pennant-wise from a line strung between plane trees in the square. Rusting play equipment, graffiti-carved benches, an agreeably beat and serene East European quality. There are panhandlers, pamphleteers, a man wearing a green forage cap emblazoned with a red star who buzzes past in a costly little convertible. The square is framed by upstyle coffee shops, including a "Book-Café" devoid of books and packed with groomed *flâneurs* sipping macchiatos and chatting into cellphones. In the square itself, some deeply tanned people with rolled sleeping bags, and a jake-legged addict who informs me in Greek, "The police never set foot here and we are grateful."

I ask him if he can direct me to Notara 26, which sounds like the title of a Leon Uris thriller but is, so I learned on Lesvos, a refugee squat established and protected by the anarchists in a deserted hotel. Suddenly the man seems to have trouble understanding me. I try again in Greek. I try in English. He's backing away, shaking his head. He turns and flees.

Savour the symmetry. I'm mistaken for a refugee by the authorities on Lesvos and for a cop by a street person in Athens.

In the grotesquely lit lobby of a one-star hotel, I find the world's last Internet café: three lonely, obsolete coin-slot computers. I check my long-neglected email and blurt out twenty or thirty replies. A piece of mildly disappointing professional news triggers a gut-shot of cortisol and a wave of chagrin, as if I've gained not one iota of perspective in my time here. Or have I learned a great deal and yet somehow the education makes no difference? As I pay the emaciated concierge, he asks in English where I'm coming from. In this awful lighting, his eyes are sad sinkholes. "Lesvos," I reply. He nods slowly, his lipless mouth curling in a sneer. I wait for some bitter remark about the refugees. He says, "We drop bombs on them and then we are surprised when they flee and come here."

I nod and he tells me, "Your eyes look very tired."

"I took the night ferry from Lesvos."

"There were many *prosfyges* on the boat?"

"Hundreds."

"My daughters had to leave me, to find work in Australia. So are they not a kind of refugee too?"

I exit into the noon light—blinding after that Gothic lobby, though this is the year's weakest noon—and follow the concierge's directions to the metro. At the entrance a slender old man, almost toothless, sits against the wall busking with a nylon-string guitar. He wears a faded baseball cap with a small Greek flag over the brim. He sings beautifully, in a cracked, damaged voice. *Thelo na krypso tin alitheia,* he quavers: *I want to hide the truth.* I listen to several songs and then ask him the meaning of the repeated word *simadi*—a word I recognize but whose meaning I can't recall. He grins without teeth, says something in Greek, then in English adds hoarsely, "It means *kiss!*"

On the train heading south toward the edge of the city, I take out my mother's old primer and turn to the index, the pages there especially yellow and fret-worn. *Simadi* means not kiss but birthmark or scar.

The last carousel

I EMERGE FROM ELLINIKO STATION, LAST STOP ON THE southern line, to a flat and windswept industrial zone bisected by a six-lane highway. A few small cars and trucks doppler past at high speed. No other pedestrian in sight.

I shield my eyes against the glare and scan the distance. At the hotel they told me that from here I'd probably be able to see the tae kwon do stadium— another pile of redundant infrastructure that the International Olympic Committee, that criminal conglomerate, required the city to build for the 2004 Summer Games.

Apparently several thousand refugees are now detained there.

A few people hurry past me into the station before I stop a man in grease-soiled coveralls and ask for help. He shrugs and points vaguely. I walk south along the highway, then turn onto a side road into an industrial park—a route that would seem unpromising except for the high scaffolding of floodlights I see up ahead, bristling against the sky. But everything seems too quiet. The side road is potholed, this industrial park deserted although it's a weekday.

I reach the base of the floodlights, which tower over a soccer field carpeted with faded blue turf. The pitch is vacant except for a grey lump by the far net. It looks like heat-swollen roadkill. I lean forward, staring hard. It's only a sandbag—a weight for the base posts. Not for the first time the suffering cat has returned to mind, again with a sense that the world's endemic pain is spiking.

I turn at the sound of a car. A small white Fiat brakes, the driver's door swings open, an older woman in sunglasses and a peach track suit springs out, waving a cellphone and jabbering. I realize she's asking where the tae kwon do stadium is. "I'm looking for it myself!" I tell her, surprised.

She merely shrugs. "No one has a *clue* where this idiotic stadium is!" she says. "I have bags of clothing here for the refugee children. Hurry, get in the car."

A minute later we're out on the six-lane highway, whizzing under an overpass and then under a large sign that indicates we're heading south toward the sea. Conversation is strained owing to my lousy Greek, her refusal or inability to speak slowly, and the howling of the old Fiat Panda, all windows lowered. I do get that some of the clothing is her grandchildren's and that they helped her collect the rest.

"One fellow said maybe the refugees have been moved to a *different* stadium!" she shouts at me. "We will find out!"

She accelerates and overtakes a small car driving in the lane to her left, both cars now scooting along at eighty

kilometres an hour. She pounds her horn until the musta-
chioed driver—ardently, inaudibly singing—looks over and
rolls down his passenger window, unleashing the campy
clamour of a Greek pop song. She yells her question and
the man frowns and nods and hollers back, seemingly
engaged by the challenge but needing clarification. The
two bellow back and forth as the cars jockey, more or less
abreast, barely an arm's reach apart. Her overbite makes
it seem she's always smiling—and maybe she is.

A third car sweeps up on my side, the right lane. A
young guy with platinum-dyed hair and sunglasses pushes
his face out the window a few feet from me. "Can I help
you find something?"

"Yes," she screams, "the tae kwon do stadium!" Leaning
across my lap she ignores the road, steering blindly with
one small, blue-veined hand, repeating her question.
Astonished, alarmed and tickled all at once, I try to give
her room, pushing my nape back against the headrest,
reclining the seat a notch. To our left the driver with the
music roars good wishes through the wind tunnel formed
by the speeding, parallel cars, then slows and falls back like
an escort vehicle, mission accomplished. Now the young
guy yells that he's pretty certain the stadium is southeast
of here, along the sea, near the old airport.

She veers onto the next off-ramp, chattering optimis-
tically. But as we roll through another immense, deserted
industrial park within sight of the sea, she loses patience
and starts demanding directions again—from other drivers
when we pause for red lights or from sidewalk pedestri-
ans we screech up beside. Some of these innocents tense
and flinch, startled by the car and her yelling; all seem

flummoxed by her questions. One man knows of the stadium but thinks it's back up near the Elliniko metro. Another thinks maybe it has been torn down.

At last a security guard answers confidently. He is smoking while standing watch, to no clear purpose, over the charred remnants of what might once have been a fuel depot. The refugees, he says, are now being housed in the old Athens airport. The directions he mutters are unnecessary—we've already passed several signs indicating the airport is just ahead.

Minutes later we pull into a weed-cracked parking lot on the edge of a vast, receding hardpan of decaying tarmac. With a jolt she wedges us in between a cop cruiser and a van stamped with the logo of a Greek cable news network. "*Pame!*" she urges, squeezing out her door while I try to edge mine open without scratching the cruiser. By the time I reach her, she has popped the hatch, tugged a sporty visor over her bobbed grey hair and is hefting out a solidly crammed garbage bag. I help her with it and pull out a second bag and then, lugging both, follow her toward a chain-link gate in a fence crowned with razor wire.

The gate is guarded by a trio of cops with peak caps, fake-looking moustaches and aviator shades: extras in a picture set in a banana republic. A dozen disheartened-looking young men sit or squat along the fence. A reporter with lacquered lips and stupendous eyelashes speaks into a microphone in front of a camera and crew. Beyond the fence, scattered brakes of bamboo and scrubby trees bristle out of the runways while tumbleweeds skitter across them. What appears to be a sports stadium, soft-focused by thermals quivering off the tarmac, floats in the distance.

Away to the north, a low brutalist terminal still bears the linked-rings emblem of Olympic Airlines and, of course, the Olympic Games—a nice irony, since it was for the 2004 Games that this place was closed and a new airport built.

As the woman approaches the cops, and I follow with the bags, the journalist signals the camera crew. The camera swings toward us. It tracks us as we pass and I can feel it trained on our backs as the woman, in her peach sweatsuit and visor, addresses the cops. I try to follow the exchange. The cops seem reluctant to admit us. The listless young refugees watch from where they sit.

The woman turns to me. "He will not let us in! He will not say why!" She looks shocked, as if she's used to toppling all impediments with her vim and momentum.

"Should we wait a little?" I ask.

"Of course we must! I will keep bothering him."

But the cop raises a peremptory hand and flicks out his cellphone to take a call. He turns away, saunters back to the gate and stands talking there, ignoring us.

I walk over to the waiting young men and delve deep into my Arabic vocabulary: "*Salam.*" One of them stands up. He's at least six-four, with broad, skinny shoulders that along with his buzz cut make his head look vulnerably small. In English he offers me a smoke. His pack of Marlboros is almost empty, and it's probably his only pack. Would it be ruder to accept or refuse him? I tell him I don't smoke, which is more or less true.

"Why are you out here?" I ask. "They won't let you in?"

"We are not Syrian, Iraqi, Afghan," he says. "So, to them, we are not true refugees."

I find my plastic lighter and light his cigarette. "Where are you from?"

"You said you don't smoke!" He nods slyly at the lighter.

"I quit." Seeing he doesn't understand, I add, "I don't smoke now."

"My friends and I are from Morocco. The others, all from Yemen. They are war refugees, but for some reason"—he grins, tight-lipped—"that war is not real."

"Ah, right. Because the Saudis are our allies."

"Your allies." He blows smoke, then clears his throat. "Forgive me."

"Here"—I hand him the lighter—"what do I need it for?"

"I don't mean to be rude."

"Not at all."

"But we are eating so much shit here, you know?"

"I hope they let you in soon," I say, and my wish epitomizes a world not right in the head—one in which a detention centre can seem a sanctuary, even if it's housed in a disintegrating airport on the windy edge of a depressed city where few, if any, refugees would want their journey to end.

The woman summons me back, points down at the bags I've left there. "They say you will now be allowed in with the clothing."

"You're not coming in too?"

"It's only you," she says solemnly. (Later I will wonder if this decision was the cops' or the woman's.) "Go on!"

"OK, I'm going!"

"*Yia ta pedia!*" she calls after me, *For the children*, as if I could have forgotten.

I carry the bags through the opened gates while the camera tracks me and the reporter yammers into her mic.

A puny police car sits waiting. One of the two cops crammed into the front seats grudgingly indicates the back. I open the door, shove in the bags and crowd in after them.

For the first time since arriving in Greece, I'm in a slow-moving, almost silent, vehicle. No sound except for the winds sweeping over the defunct runways. Tumbleweeds blow past, outpacing us. We meander along a complex route dictated by scattered sinkholes, lines of rusting, buckled fence and the dusty little trees that erupt everywhere. Slowly the stadium grows larger. Glancing in the rear-view I judge that the driver, looking straight ahead through mirrored sunglasses, will not welcome any questions or comments.

Over the decades before this site was abandoned, many millions will have passed through here, including me, travelling with my parents and baby sister to visit my mother's extended family half a century ago. (A century, it turns out, is a tiny thing.) I am four years old. We disembark from a DC-8 and walk across this very tarmac in the torrid July heat and squeeze into the cherry-red convertible of my mother's second cousin—a playboy with connections—parked on the edge of the runway. *I have dealt with the customs agents—it is no problem!* Such is my remembrance. I know it could be fictive—compounded of snapshots, embellished family yarns, the memories of memories—yet the episode is not implausible, not for Greece in the 1960s.

Some minutes later, the silent cops and I skirt a reef of prickly pear sprouting out of the tarmac and stop in front of the hulking stadium, presumably another Olympics boondoggle. I squirm out of the back seat, grappling with the garbage bags. "*Eucharisto,*" I thank the men. "And will I return with you?"

The driver doesn't answer or even look toward me as he pulls away.

I stand at the foot of the stadium, my arms pulled taut by the heavy bags. The high concrete facade, presumably just over a decade old, is already mottled and cracking. I mount the front steps and enter a dank, drafty atrium. Directly ahead a stairway climbs to the next level. Receding on either hand are long narrow concrete rooms with camp cots tightly ranked, as in a field hospital.

In the doorless doorway of one of these wards I stand frozen. Embrasures in the bunker-thick walls admit light but no air. On each cot a person lies, sometimes two, a parent and child. Small tents sag among the cots. People curl on blankets on the floor. The smell of unwashed bodies and clothing is dense.

A girl lies separate, skinny, pregnant, barely a teenager. From the cots, faces listlessly watch me; the girl, maybe one of those raped by the traffickers or by other refugees, stares too, then lets her eyelids fall shut.

I walk deeper into the stadium's concrete catacombs in search of help, passing other dim, cramped, smelly rooms. No sign of a shower or even a sink. No sign of food. When I see an open doorway filled with sunlight I rush over like a man who has been trapped underground for days. I drop the bags at the threshold, step out into the light and look down across a pristine, Prussian-blue soccer field. Its markings look fresh, its goals have whitewashed posts and bright orange netting; everything is spookily new, as if unused since 2004. On the far side, under gleaming empty bleachers, some refugee men and children kick a ball around. I would join them in a minute if I could. Beyond the bleachers, a swath of eroding tarmac where a relic DC-9 decays into the runway; a brownbelt of urban sprawl; a culminating tier of low treeless mountains.

"Can I help you?"

I turn around. A young but faded redhead with a freckled nose and twitchy, pale eyes offers to show me to the storage room. I smell the gum she's rapidly chewing—spearmint. She's from Kansas, she says, and though I've just stepped out of a black-and-white world into sunlit Technicolor, I resist the obvious quip. She swings one of the bags up onto her shoulder with a strength that seems manic, adrenalized. "Heavy! This stuff wet or just packed tight? Doesn't matter, doesn't matter, we need it. This way, come on."

We reach the storage room—locked. I peer through a window into a depot full of cardboard boxes and plastic bins brimming over with clothes and footwear. Piled along a wall are scores of garbage bags spilling pants, shirts, parkas, shoes. "Weird!" says the woman, swinging the bag back down. As I try the handle again, a second woman appears, also young but taller, high-chinned, exuding territorial authority.

"The door is locked for a *reason*," she says in a husky voice, Greek accent. "We have too many clothes donated, too few volunteers to sort them. We don't want these bags."

I try to make eye contact but her hard gaze keeps drilling into my forehead.

"Why not just put them aside for when you run out?" I ask.

"We shall not run out. We have far too much." The smartphone clenched in her hand goes off and she glances

down at it, talking over the ringtone, the shrill crescendo
of the *Titanic* love theme. "We have clothing enough for
months here. The local people are too generous."

"But the refugees will keep coming, right?"

"We have far too much—take them back!" She claps the
phone to her ear, turns and strides away, heels smacking
the concrete.

The woman from Kansas leans in, exhaling mint, and
murmurs, "Drive the stuff to Notara 26, maybe? The anarchist place? I don't know. I wish I knew."

"Are there still people at the tae kwon do stadium?" I ask.

"It got too crowded, too dirty. They shut it down. Two
days ago. I was there, believe me, it was hellish. They're all
being brought here now. Kind of like a fresh start?" She air-
quotes "fresh" and flicks another tab of gum—it's nicotine
gum, I see—into her mouth.

I start back toward the main doors with the two bags,
which feel heavier by the moment—a weight not merely
physical. I can't seriously think of returning the clothes
to the Greek *yiayia* who has been trying all day to deliver
them, and who may have spent many more days collecting
them. Reaching the atrium, I consider backtracking to the
storage room and depositing the bags against the locked
door. Then an impulse grips me. After looking around, I
mount the stairs two at a time, hefting the bags high and
clear, catching my breath on the landing.

To either side lie cinder-block wards jammed with silent
figures sprawled on cots or on the floor. I'm not used to
seeing refugees look this languid and defeated. Even in the
gulag of Moria—where some of these people must have

stayed just days or weeks ago—there was a feeling of energy, initiative, hope.

So it seems now in comparison.

Choosing randomly (what else can I do?) I enter a room: a lanky, winded Saint Nicholas bearing Christmas gift bags. On a hammocked cot, two toddlers lie furled together like twins in utero. I call out softly, "Does anyone here speak English?"

A woman, pregnant, stands and glides toward me, her feet hidden by her abaya. "I speak a little." Her features are delicate, pale and serenely sad. Generations of Orthodox ikon painters have been faithfully depicting her, chapel by chapel, as if forecasting her arrival on a Greek island and eventual confinement in this dystopia, where she might well give birth.

Her baby the future made flesh.

I struggle to unknot a bag and then, swearing under my breath, *fuck, come on!*, I claw and rip it open. "Clothing for the kids!" I announce in a bright, breaking voice, holding up a miniature hoodie the tangerine colour of a life vest. "Please, share them out?"—I circle my finger in the clammy air—"and give the rest to people in the other rooms. OK?" She lays a hand over her heart and shakes her head, *sorry, don't understand*, so I repeat the words, holding up the pathetic hoodie and miming the act of passing it around. As others rise off their cots and approach, I retreat and back out the doorway, women from other rooms jostling in past me.

I run down the stairs and out into the sun, its welcome warmth and obliviating white glare. After the stadium's penitential crowding, greyness and stasis, this tundra of tarmac is a relief, cleansing as a desert vista. *Take the clothing back… we are too few!* The volunteer chief was as frostily officious as any NGO wonk, but—ask yourself this again—would you have been willing to serve *here* for a month instead of in and around Mithymna?

The little police car is not waiting. I'd have been surprised if it was. In the distance, near the gated entrance, small figures in a long file are tramping in toward the stadium. I set out for the entrance. For some minutes I wind around outcrops of cactus pear and bamboo and tamarisk and the lapsing fences, yet that line of marching figures gets no closer. In the heat thermals welling off the tarmac they seem to float over the earth, their feet treading water. But then, in short order, as if they've gained traction or I have, we're about to meet.

Their straggling line extends all the way back to the gate. At the front of the line, humping backpacks or garbage bags, it's the dozen Moroccans and Yemenis who were told they would not be admitted. The tall one I spoke to before gives me a cocky grin, as pleased as if he has talked his way, ticketless, into a rock concert. Again he pushes his cigarette pack toward me and this time I take one—his second last. He lights it with my old lighter. "Good luck on your journey," I say and he claps a hand over his heart, inclining his buzz-cut head, then strides on as if eager to regain his place at the front.

My legs feel heavy as I pass the steadily filing queue— young men first and then families, the children holding their parents' hands. We exchange waves and smiles while I smoke the Moroccan kid's shitty cigarette and make for the exit with a queasy stomach.

Good luck on your journey!

I reach the open gate through which refugees are still streaming in. Several reporters now stand talking in front of camera crews. The police ignore me—the one person exiting while hundreds enter. There are now several grimy old tour buses lined up in the parking lot, but, as before, only a few cars. The Greek donor's white Fiat is not among them. I ask one of the cops whether he saw her leave. Not looking at me, trying to count the refugees as they pass, he says, "Who knows? We are all busy. She left."

But weren't we here at the gate just a half-hour ago, an hour at most? I check my watch, though I'm not sure what time we arrived. The sun does seem lower in the sky than it should and the shadows far longer.

As I walk out toward the road, I pass a man tending a small fire of twigs and plastic bottles. He sits within a few steps of a parked squad car. Nobody seems to notice or care. Grizzled, gap-toothed, he leers like a friendly drifter in a dust bowl hobo camp.

I stand by the road that runs along the Saronic Gulf but there is no traffic at all now, no potential rides. But just up the road and on the other side is a tram stop. I look to the southeast. In the distance, gilded by the low sun, a tram appears. I run up the road, cross to the silent stop and try to buy a ticket from the machine. The credit card slot is taped over. Coins just rattle through into the return.

I glance down the tracks: the tram has made little progress. Not far up the line I can see another stop. I jog along the tracks for a couple of minutes and climb the steps onto the platform. Another broken dispenser. I look back. The tram has gained on me but only a little, as if it too is damaged.

As I run along the tracks toward the next stop, a stretch of deserted beach opens to my left, down below. It recedes in a long golden curve to the northwest, toward capes and mountains whose contours and collective aspect are eerily familiar, as if recently dreamed.

Of course.

I reach the third stop and abuse another extinct ticket dispenser, *useless piece of shit*, and all at once the tram is bearing down on me, in fact moving swiftly, in uncanny silence. I turn to flag it. It's not slowing, so I gesture at the ticket machine and splay my hands. No driver visible through the sun-mirroring windshield. On the panel above it, pixeled Greek and English words are scrolling like a stock market newsfeed: ΕΚΤΟΣ ΛΕΙΤΟΥΡΓΕΙΑ... NOT IN SERVICE... ΕΚΤΟΣ ΛΕΙΤΟΥΡΓΕΙΑ...

After the tram whispers past and then swings inland along the tracks and up toward the city, I notice the name of this stop. I read it again and then I say it out loud. *Paralia Glyfadas.* Yes... Glyfada Beach... it was somewhere right around here that I stayed with my family almost fifty years ago. I step down off the platform, walk toward the water, stop on a low bluff and look up the coast. The sun is about half an hour above the sea. The spectral midway spread out below, with its skeletal rides and rusting Ferris wheel... I don't remember it, but beyond the last carousel there's a marina—boatless, closed for the season or out of business— and it looks right.

Somewhere along this empty arc of beach, among those now-dated cabanas and low-rise hotels, we waded hand in hand into the August-thronged shallows, my mother half the age that I am now. I am pointing at things and asking her to teach me the Greek word: that blue-painted dinghy that a brown old man is rowing among the anchored sailboats... *Varka,* she says, distractedly, already displaying that vague incuriosity about her mother tongue that will deepen over the years ahead.

I think she wanted to leave her Greek life behind, at least partly—to marry and then merge into a world that promised, among other things, peaceful amnesia, an insulated suburbanity far from the old world with its tribes and strictures, collective demands, heritable grudges of ancient standing. Instead: the fencelessly flowing yards of a new subdivision, the bland chatter of cocktail-calm neighbours in the soft twilight, the shouts of children off somewhere playing cops and robbers or war in perfect safety, the white noise of sprinklers on weedless lawns. A place where vices, rages and bad smells are suppressed or decently contained. Grief or exultation likewise. Death above all. Most folks white, in fact WASP, straight, courteous, middle-class. A near-theological belief in the existence of Normal. The complacent, depraved fantasy of being the nicest, or the greatest, nation on earth, far from the weaponized frontiers where crazy shit goes down.

Who could blame her or any of them?

She must not have been surprised when, soon after our visit, a military cabal seized power in Greece. Or when that junta's interference in Cyprus (brokered and abetted by the CIA) triggered a war that led to ethnic cleansing and created a hundred thousand refugees. Had she still been alive in 2008, she would not have been surprised by Greece's economic crisis or, later, the arrival on its shores of wave after wave of Syrians, Iraqis, Afghans and others, whom the impoverished Greeks would somehow have to help and house.

But to hear of refugees and migrants starting to trickle north across Canada's famously undefended border, and to hear of how, along a busier border far to the south, children and parents would be forcibly parted in scenes of the kind she would have associated with the past, the bad old Balkans, the Middle East... these things might have surprised her. Such deeds don't happen here. (They've always happened here.) As for 9/11, as she lay dying, the news—the looping images she would have glimpsed fleetingly if at all—must have fused into her drugged delirium, those jets the same ones that thundered low over our suburb in the 1970s, taking off from or descending into Toronto's international airport.

Everyone gets away with certain things for a while but no one gets away with everything forever. This stretch of coast, from carousel to sunset, exudes a sense that the game is up, the party over, illusions played out. Then again, if our illusions are harmful, isn't disillusionment a *good* thing, a necessary correction so painful that our word for it is negative? Nobody ever changes until they have to. I walk uphill along the tracks toward the city with the year's weakest sun warming my back.

AFTERWORD

I'D HOPED THAT IF I HAD TO ADD ONE OF THESE, IT would report that the situation on Lesvos had resolved or greatly improved; that a war in Syria was not continuing to push waves of refugees into Turkey and toward the sealed borders of Europe; that Moria, the main refugee camp on the island, was no longer desperately crowded.

On the day I was there, in December, 2015, Moria held some 3000 people. It was hard to imagine the former military base, with its capacity of around 1000, accommodating many more. Yet as of now, there are some 20,000 refugees in a version of the camp that is only slightly larger, and mainly because it has spilled out beyond its walls. Many more people are headed there now, pushed across the Turkish-Greek border straits by a country no longer willing to host them and toward a country equally unwilling—because barely able—to take them.

As for the islanders, five years of disruption and hardship have exhausted their *philoxenia*; aid workers and journalists are no longer welcome there either.

And now, a pandemic.

Thich Nhat Hanh has argued that hope is a tragic distraction, but he might agree that hopelessness is even worse. Can we observers somehow lodge in the space between the two—the one place where useful, urgent action is possible?

—*S.H., Kingston, June 2020*

ACKNOWLEDGEMENTS

I'VE BEEN LUCKY TO WORK WITH JOHN METCALF AGAIN, some thirty years after first encountering his renowned editing style: sympathetic and yet uncompromisingly tough. When he first read the manuscript that became *Reaching Mithymna*, he vowed to push me until the book was right, out of respect, he said, for the dignity and struggle of the refugees.

Ginger Pharand's sharp eye and sensitive ear have likewise been invaluable.

Dan Wells of Biblioasis: thank you. Ditto Vanessa Stauffer, Chloe Moore, and John Sweet.

The artist and activist who inspired the Jack Marvin character, Neal McQueen, read the proofs of this book before agreeing to let Biblioasis use his photographs. In an email, he explained to me that he recently received a diagnosis of Asperger's syndrome. With no undertone of grievance, he pointed out that, lacking knowledge of his diagnosis, I might have misinterpreted some of his words and attitudes, or misattributed to him the negative remarks of others.

I thank also Jamal Saeed (who is not responsible for the gender error in the phrase *wahid eayila*, which volunteers mistakenly used in Moria), and Mary Huggard, Elena Heighton, Alexander Scala, Nicole Winstanley, Merilyn Simonds, Karen Connelly, Bernie Covo, Neal McQueen, Jennifer Warren, and Shelley Tanaka of Groundwood Books (who has given Kanella, the OXY camp stray, a second home).

Steven Heighton's most recent books are a novel, *The Nightingale Won't Let You Sleep*, which has appeared in French and Ukrainian translations and has been optioned for film, and a poetry collection, *The Waking Comes Late*, which received the 2016 Governor General's Award for Poetry.

His novel *Afterlands* has appeared in six countries; was a *New York Times Book Review* editors' choice and was cited on year-end lists in the USA, the UK, and Canada; and is in pre-production for film. His short fiction and poetry have received four gold National Magazine Awards and have appeared in *London Review of Books*, *Granta*, *Best English Stories*, *Poetry*, *Best American Poetry*, *Tin House*, *Agni*, *Best American Mystery Stories*, *Zoetrope*, *New England Review*, and five editions of *Best Canadian Stories*.

Heighton has been nominated for the Governor General's Award, the Trillium Award, and Britain's W.H. Smith Award, and he is an occasional fiction reviewer for the *New York Times Book Review*.